THE DAY I MET MY

BOAZ

A POWERFUL STORY THAT WILL GIVE YOU THE COURAGE TO BELIEVE IN REAL LOVE

Keci Monique'

I love my
Boaz

To the woman who just received this book:

I want to personal thank you for your purchase The Day I Met My Boaz. My prayer is that you are as blessed as I was when I began my journey writing about meeting my Boaz. I pray for your journey to healing, overcoming, and that you, as the WHOLE WOMAN, will be blessed to find the love that you desire as a result of making a choice to do your work.

Many Blessings To You!

ISBN: 979-8-63886-517-7 (Paperback)

Library of Congress Control Number: 2020913621

Any references to real people, other than my husband and myself, are used fictitiously. Names, characters, and places are products real and the author has experienced, visited, and/or encountered them.

Front cover image by Keci Monique`
Book design by Keci Monique`

First printing edition 2020.

HarLa Reyn Publishing
589 Palisade Drive
Brunswick, GA 31523

www.therughtfactor.org
www.harlareynpublishing.com

DEDICATION

The Day I Met My Boaz is dedicated to the women who have not had success with their relationships as a result of traumatic experiences that have taken place in your lives. Sometimes, we are left to feel like we aren't good enough, we aren't worthy, we're not pretty enough, too fat, too skinny, too old, and so many other things that society says is wrong that makes us not admirable of being in a productive relationship. On top of experiencing trauma, you fail to gain the acceptance of someone you were hoping would be your forever love. Somewhere in this, the trauma that you have experienced has caused feelings of abandonment, rejection, and even depression and anxiety.

I am here to tell you that you are not alone. I am also here to tell you that your past is not your final destination. You have the ability to rewrite your destiny. Grab your pen, journal, and of course, this book and lets change the trajectory of your lives.

To God Be The Glory!

THE MOST DIFFICULT PART
ABOUT RELATIONSHIPS IS
REALIZING THAT YOU ARE
NOT IN THE SAME SEASON
WITH THE CONTENDER!

Keci Monique`

v

EPIGRAPH

It's Not Who You Love, but What You Love

The Bible presents marriage as an institution that should be highly respected and esteemed above all other institutions. Hebrews 13:4 says, "Marriage should be honored by all, and the marriage bed kept pure, for God will judge the adulterer and all the sexually immoral." The King James Version reads, "Marriage is honorable in all..." "Honorable" translates the Greek word timios, which also means "valuable, costly, honored, esteemed, beloved, and precious." All means "all": The Greek word is pas, meaning "all, any, every, the whole, thoroughly, whatsoever, and whosoever." Marriage, then, should be valued and esteemed, and held in highest honor at all times in all things by all people everywhere. That is God's design.

Dr. Myles Munroe

TABLE OF CONTENTS

15 | The Day I Met My Boaz

23 | Mr. Dressed Up In Lies

31 | Mr. Totally Ambivalent

42 | Mr. Love Pistol

53 | The Emotional Pain

66 | The Excellent Plan

71 | The Process

79 | The Purpose

83 | My Boaz

Our Vow Renewal: July 30th, 2016

I married him a second time.

If I could, I would marry him every day.

FOREWARD

The authoress, Mrs. Keci Monique` Reynolds and I, have been friends for over 20 years. We have cried, laughed, argued, and shared many experiences that allows us to maintain a relationship which resembles the true essence of sisterhood. Her story of triumph while having living through tragedy is a compelling one that I am sure will touch the heart of many. Although she had to kiss plenty of frogs before finding her prince, her story is one that is shared amongst many women as they journey through the torturous path towards finding true love. I believe in that process and that she came to understand that true love was love of self, first. It was only when she began to truly love herself and put herself first that her Boaz appeared.

I would like to add that I was instrumental in helping her to recognize, her now husband, was her Boaz from the very beginning. As the story goes, Jerome and Keci were Facebook Friends. He would comment on everything Keci would post. She could have typed the word "boo" and there he was in the comment section liking the comment and making sure to speak on her posts. I mentioned this to Keci and she quickly blew him off and stated that he was probably after the wrong thing. In her words, "He is probably all up in the club, skirt chasing, with a gang of baby mommas, and a mouth full of gold teeth." At the time, she was working on her graduate degree in Forensic Psychology. She criminally profiled him in a stereotypical way. Of course, the more he made himself known, Keci had no choice but to take notice. Once she gave him a chance the relationship quickly blossomed from a friendship to a romantic relationship and the two became inseparable.

They are definitely a match made in heaven. I believe that the love of self, caused Keci to heal many parts of her life that some might consider fractured. She sought counseling from God and a Christian counselor and was able to reflect on how a lifetime of abandonment and abuse had affected her relationships with men and relationships in her family, and even with some friends. In the end, after a lifetime of agony, anguish, and abuse, Keci was able to discover self-healing. It was then that she knew that Jerome was her first and only true love. This book has the ability to help may women who have had similar circumstances that Keci experienced throughout her life. In the end, she is a source of hope and inspiration to us all.

Dr. Kimberly D. Dixon

PREFACE

The contents recorded in this book are true and real occurrences. I am thankful to my Almighty God, who I know, without a shadow of a doubt, kept His promise to never leave me and never forsake me through it all.

I can sit back and take the woe is me road to complaining and never make a move in the best direction or I can take the higher road with ALL that I have gone through and use it to empower others.

Take my experiences and learn from them, shift your viewpoint, discover new aspects of life that are the hidden jewels to discovering your way to having Serenity in your Relationship.

Keci Monique

To my beautiful husband:

Thank you for teaching me the true meaning of love. You are always supporting me in every endeavor that I set out to conquer. You have exemplified Boaz and the Ephesians 5:23. Your calm spirit and extra cool demeanor helps to keep me grounded so that I can focused on striving for our goals. You are truly the best part of me. I love you with every breath that God has given me for you. You are my superhero.

Acknowledgements

1. To My Sister, from another mother and another mister:

There is so much that I can say about our laughs, our cries and all of the times in between. You have been my rock even when you didn't or couldn't understand what storm I was going through. No matter what this life brings, I will always remember your faithfulness, loyalty and how you gave me your shoulder to lean on. I must give back now because someone will need my shoulder. Thank you for being a strong pillar in my life. I love you my unbiological sister.

2. To My Sister, from another mother and another mister:

The words that you uttered to me over the years never fell on the deaf ears. You have given me your wisdom, love, and your heart through everything that you inculcated. You have had my back in times when I had no one else to turn to. You always said to me, "When niggas do what's best for them, they are doing what's best for you." I didn't understand it at the tender age of 23 years old. But when I did understand it, I ran with it and I live by it until this day. Thank you for being a strong pillar in my life. Unconditionally, I love you my unbiological sister.

To My Cousin, Jenee´:

I am FOREVER thankful for September 26th, 2010. If you hadn't made that post, even though you were dealing with something heavy, I probably wouldn't have met my Boaz. I remember asking you if you had ever dated him. if you had previously dated him, all bets were about to be off. When you answered, "No," it made my day. You told me what a good guy he is and that you believed that he would make me happy. Not only has he made me happy, but he has also been more than what I ever imagined a husband could ever be. Thank you cousin for that night.

To the two ladies who pushed me to inquire about My Boaz:

Thank you for those eyes on my posts. You kept asking me, "Who is Jerome Reynolds?" Although I had no clue at the time, you pressed me to find out. I am so glad that I did. He asked me for my phone number and that first phone call was everything. It was the prelude to our always and forever.

To my auntie Linda . . .

Although you are no longer here with me in the physical, you will forever be in my heart. God blessed us with almost four beautiful years together. Your unfailing love for me, your unconditional love for me, and your presence in my life made me want to do better. You taught me love can make a difference in the way someone thrives. You showed me that someone is only limited by what they limit themselves to.

The talks that we had, the laughs, and some cries bonded us together in a way no one ever understood. I love the fact that you understood me. You cared for me. You never judged me. You never questioned my integrity. You always supported me. You were always honest with me, even if I didn't like it. You never treated me different or as an outsider. That is what I love most about you. Your heart was so big. You held so many in there. When you showed me that there was room in there for me, I knew that you were not only my auntie, but my friend. You became my strength and my serenity.

I write this dedication to you to let you know your love still lives in me.

I love you auntie Linda,
Until we meet again...

To my gran'mommy & gran'daddy . . .

One of the most precious jewels that children can have is a grandmother and grandfather who loves them with their ENTIRE heart. You were an AMAZING woman who exemplified the essence of a good wife. You spent 42 awesome years with my gran'daddy, who I loved dearly. I am thankful to God for blessing me with the both of you.

Because of the love and marriage that you had, I am totally inspired to be the wife that I have been called to be. Thank you for showing me what love is and love among the married.

I love you both...
Until we meet again...

INTRODUCTION

The Day I Met My Boaz is the day that I found Serenity in my relationship. I was at a point in my life where I had a conversation with God and let Him know that I was alright with being single. I had gotten to the point that I was okay with just me. I set myself up for celibacy and was on my journey to falling in love with me. This type of falling in love in much different from a romantic falling in love.

Falling in love with yourself means that you are willing to do what you need to do to establish healthy boundaries, say no and/or walking away from toxic relationships and letting it be alright, forgive to set yourself free, own your part in every situation and do positive and constructive things to build you and make you happy.

Within two weeks of saying this to God, I met the man who became my Boaz. I wasn't looking for anyone when he approached me. I literally wasn't interested in a relationship with any man, especially a long distance one. My friends kept seeing that he was liking my posts on social media. They continuously asked me about him. I soon found out that he was not only my soulmate, he became my best friend, my husband, my lover, and companion.

Although my Serenity started within myself, it was highly enhanced when we decided to be together in a relationship. As I write this book, I am thankful for most blissful years of my life. We are nine years in, with eight years of marriage and forever to go.

CHAPTER ONE

The Day I Met My Boaz

The day I met my Boaz was nothing short of God's glory. For many years I was informed that I would know that I know when the right one comes along. I was at a pivotal point in my life where everything needed change. I was working a good job. I had a lovely townhome that I was renting in Corona Hills, California. I was driving a Lexus, even though it was an older model, it was mine. My money was flowing fluidly. Aside from all of the material possessions, I dug deep to do the work that was needed to move onto the mountain top of the relationships that I had experienced. I literally came up on the rough side of the mountain. I was doing my best to make it in.

Understand this, The Day I Met My Boaz is not a fairytale in the traditional way. I am not selling you a pipe dream to make you believe that I woke up like this. I did not wake up in the arms of my Boaz and life was grandiose along the way. I will be transparent with you. I want you to understand that there is no fast way to a successful relationship without doing the work. Doing the work is mandatory to get to your mountain top of relationship bliss. If you do not do the work required, you will find yourself chasing your tail like a puppy. Chasing your tail is an idiom. An idiom is an expression that typically presents a metaphorical, non-literal meaning attached to the phrase or statement. In essence, the term "chase your tail" means to take action that is ineffectual and does not lead to progress. Refers to how a dog can exhaust itself by chasing its own tail (Farlex Dictionary of Idioms, 2015). Therefore, if you are trying to achieve relationship success, you want to reach that relationship mountain top, you want relationship serenity and you want to leave the relationship drama behind, then this book is for you.

If you have had a tumultuous time in your relationships, experienced rejection, and abandonment in your relationships (this is not limited to romantic relationships), or if you have no blueprint for relationship success, grab your tissue, purchase the journal and let's get ready to do this.

Meeting My Boaz was what I needed when I needed it. After doing the work that I needed to do to accomplish my goals of rebuilding my relationship with Christ, I wasn't looking for a relationship. I got to the point where I was prepared to ride this ride solo. Years prior, I remember the Holy Spirit enlightening me about cutting my hair. He said that my husband to be liked long hair. My hair was a decent length at this time. However, I was prepared to cut it and start over fresh. Lorella Flego (2016), said,

"A dramatic change of a hairstyle, new hair colour or just some highlights reflect our subconscious wish for changes. When we want to turn the page to a new chapter in our life, we start at the head. Sometimes an unpleasant experience is the reason, like an end of a relationship, death of a loved one or something else significant. We get rid of the pain in our past symbolically by cutting our hair and changing our hairstyle that somehow ties us to it. A woman with long hair is considered beautiful and attractive. Long, silky and shiny hair touch the deepest parts of human psyche: healthy hair is attractive because it represents health, youth and fertility. Although it's true that this perception varies depending on the culture. The Maasai people consider a woman with a shaved head or extremely short hair to be beautiful. The Native American tribe of Navajo believed that hair is the part of the body that is closest to thoughts. So to them, long hair was a representation of memory. Even Coco Chanel said: "A woman who cuts her hair is planning changes in her life." Hair actually symbolizes our identity, it's linked to Eros, to a growing desire that needs some direction. That is why it's so pleasant when somebody strokes our hair."

16

I was in search of a deeper change that no longer tied me to the yokes of bondage of failed, broken, abandoned, and rejected relationships. While I worked on my inner woman, I was looking for a newness on my outer woman. Short hair was going to be the way. I was planning on relocating back to Georgia. I wanted to buy a BMW 700 Series. I knew I didn't want to buy any property in California because it was too expensive. Honestly, I didn't want to buy property outside of being married. My thought was that I wanted my biggest purchases to be with my husband. This doesn't mean that a woman shouldn't pursue property ownership on her own. It wasn't something that I wanted to do. Nonetheless, I had already started looking for employment in Georgia. I wanted to move to Newnan, Georgia. I prayed about it and talked to God about it. I started writing my plans on paper. In Habakkuk 2:2-4 (NKJV) talks about The Just Live by Faith.

Then the Lord answered me and said:
"Write the vision
And make it plain on tablets,
That he may run who reads it.
For the vision is yet for an appointed time;
But at the end it will speak, and it will not lie.
Though it tarries, wait for it;
Because it will surely come,
It will not tarry.
"Behold the proud,
His soul is not upright in him;
But the just shall live by his faith.

However, in planning, Proverbs 16:9 (TLB) says that we should make plans—counting on God to direct us. So let's examine: I was preparing to move back to Georgia. I was searching for employment. In my preparing, I needed to write the vision and make it plain. I needed to be patient and wait for the appointed time. On top of this, I needed to maintain my faith in God, especially since eminent changes had taken place in my life. I was not going to go backwards. There was no quitting. There was no returning to my past. Understandably, you want to reach your mountain top of relationship bliss. You can. However, you can't skip the process to get there. If that were the case, we'd all be billionaires, have the bomb.com relationships, and there would be no need for you to read my book. Therefore, take everything that you learn here and do the work needed to overcome your challenges. If you try to skip this part, just know that you will have to repeat portions, if not all, of the processes to get to where you are trying to go. Remember, the dog who chases his tail never gets any further than that. I want you to be whole and healed. I want you to come out of the lion's den never smelling like the fire or hell that you have been through but smelling like a rose. Roses are beautiful flowers that have long been a symbol of love. According to an article by Linda Crampton (2020), roses belong to the genus Rosa, which exists in both wild and cultivated forms. A rose color can have a different meaning for different people. Often people like a color simply because it's beautiful. It's fun to look at the traditional meanings of the colors, though.

- Red: romantic love
- Pink: gratitude and appreciation
- Orange: desire and passion
- Yellow: friendship
- Lavender: enchantment or love at first sight
- White: innocence or purity of love
- Black: pure elegance
- Royal blue: True love associated with the unattainable
- Royal purple: mysticism, royalty, and love

Today, red roses are a frequent symbol of true love and are a traditional Valentine's Day gift. In the past, white roses were used to symbolize love. Even today, the white flowers are often referred to as "bridal roses" and are used at weddings. They're also used to express love for a deceased person at a funeral. You can make it through this. You can come through the fire smelling like a rose. Don't doubt yourself through this, but trust God for everything to see you through while you are doing the work.

Whatever you lacked prior to reading this book, let that all be a thing of the past. Your mother wasn't there for you growing up. Neither was mine. Your

mother was a drug addict. So was mine. Your mother was a fille de joie. So was mine. Your father wasn't there for you neither was mine. Your father got married or is in a relationship with a woman who doesn't care for his children that he had before her. Same here sis. You always felt rejected by everyone in life. My hand is raised. You were abandoned by your village. Both of my hands are raised. What I am saying here is that there is no excuse. So what because you didn't have the blueprint to life. So what because your parents failed. We all do. WHAT ARE YOU GOING TO DO WITH ALL OF THE WEALTH OF CHALLENGES THAT YOU HAVE BEARED IN THIS LIFE? You may have lost your mother or father at an early age. You may have experienced some violent acts against you from family, partners, or strangers. You may have or had a relationship with a married man. ←
Let this go sis. He ain't yours and he NEVER will be. Regardless of the fact, you have the power to move into a new season in your life if you want it. Meeting My Boaz, a worthy man, as the bible calls him, was not by chance. God didn't drop him out of the sky. I wasn't lucky. God didn't deliver him on a silver platter although that would have been nice.

After working on me, breaking soul ties, yokes of bondage, abandonment and rejection issues and having such low self-esteem, God presented us to one another. Actually, I was presented to him. it was very non-traditional. I was not interested, initially. Remember, I was ready to ride solo and cut my hair off and buy a BMW 700 Series and move back to Georgia. The moment was amazing. We actually took over the conversation that was started by my cousin, Jenee'. He was persistent, but very kind and subtle. He was smooth. He knew what he wanted. He came for me. He made it known that he did.

How this unfolded for me was in the recognition of the work that I did to improve myself for myself and ultimately, for the glory of God. I was ready for marriage and I was done with the single life. You can't have both. It causes a lot of confusion. I knew that I was one woman who wanted only one man. I wanted to date him, marry him, and date him for the rest of our lives. I established boundaries that I refused to bend on. I established my 80/20 Rule and refused to bend on it. I recognized that my relationships suffered because I never knew how to be in a relationship. My relationships suffered because my parents didn't know how to teach me to be in a relationship. They didn't have it within themselves to give me. Instead of focusing on what I didn't have or get from my parents, which was a lot. A lot of my life skills suffered for lack of knowledge. Hosea 4:6 (ESV) My people are destroyed for lack of knowledge. Because you have rejected knowledge, I reject you from being a priest to me. And since you have forgotten the law of your God, I also will forget your children. I was suffering. Although the devil meant for these situations to break me, God sought to turn it around for my good. Genesis 50:20 (NIV) You intended to harm me, but God intended it for good to accomplish what is now being done, the saving of many lives. We are presented with many opportunities in life. It is up to us to accept or reject the opportunity. Sometimes we take these opportunities and get the best prize out of it. Other times we take these chances and they turn out bad, dangerous and in some cases with a loss of life. I urge you more than anything else, put God's work first and do what he wants. Then the other things will be yours as well, Matthew 6:33 (CEV). Choose wisely in whatever you do.

If you want to discover your way to finding your Boaz, just know that it all begins with you. If you keep the mindset that you are who you are and someone will just have to accept you like you are then you will continue to end up in the same scenarios that have haunted you since you began dating or whenever life took it's turn for the worse with your relationships. If you want better, not only do you have to do better, you have to change from the inside first. One thing that is definitely true, you won't have to go looking for your Boaz, he will find you in due time. It's an act of faith and you still have to add work with it. This man is not going to drop out of the sky. Remember Habakkuk 2:3 (NKJV) - For the vision is yet for an appointed time; But at the end it will speak, and it will not lie. Though it tarries, wait for it; Because it will surely come, It will not tarry. Therefore, while you are waiting, do your work so that you will be ready and won't have to get ready.

The storyline is discussing three men I dated and one man I married. I call them Mr. Dressed Up In Lies, Mr. Totally Ambivalent, Mr. Love Pistol, and

My Boaz. Their names literally tell their story. As you prepare to read, I want to encourage you to get your tissue, grab your coffee and get ready to laugh. While reading, if you notice any resemblances to your life, do not hesitate to feel it. Even if you see something that is resemblance of someone else you know, get them involved and tell them to grab a copy for themselves. My goal is to help you to see it, acknowledge it, deal with it, heal from it, grow from it, and move into a new place in your life. Most of us have dated some not so Mr. or Mrs. Right for Me type of men before. As you read about these three men, you might get angry. You might laugh out loud. You might feel my past pain. You might even be going through it right now. Either way, I pray that you enjoy this book and that you have some great takeaways from it.

Dear Heavenly Father,

I pray for each person reading this book that you blessed me to birth. I pray that everyone who is trying to figure it out will see value in this book will be able to find the missing pieces to their puzzle in order to put their lives back together. I pray for everyone who is or has dealt with abandonment, rejection, depression, anxiety, PTSD, and any other negative emotion or mental issue as it relates to relationships. I ask that you impart wisdom, knowledge, and understanding to them. Give them the strength to do their work. Give them the mindset to choose to love themselves and to command their atmosphere in areas where they have been weak. Give each person the ability to see themselves as You see them: loved, whole, the ABSOLUTE best, healed, successful in their relationships with people, relationship serenity, the ability to love despite past trauma, and most of all, that each woman will be able to marry her Boaz and each man will be able to find and marry his Ruth. As I am praying this prayer, I ask that you give them the ability not to settle and not to compromise. Let them move into their winning season for love under new management. I ask these and more in the matchless name of Jesus. Amen.

CHAPTER TWO

Mr. Dressed Up in Lies

Mr. Dressed Up in Lies is a suave individual with charisma who is educated and claimed to have so much going on. He was a businessman who always had a bunch of meetings that he attended and facilitated throughout the day... EVERYDAY, including Saturday and Sunday. We talked on most days, but it wasn't' for long. He always gave the excuse of having a meeting to attend. He dressed up his lies as good as he dressed himself. he never followed through on anything that he promised. In fact, during one of our on again times in the relationship, he said, "I have an engagement ring for you, but you don't deserve it." He knew that I wanted to be married. I didn't want the one day. I wanted the whole she'bang-bang. The question remained if I wanted this with him. some days I thought I did. He was loving at times. Then there were other times when he seemed to be uncouthed. Hence the fact that we were on and off for three years.

I received promise after promise of how he was saving money for our wedding. He went back and forth about how I didn't deserve the engagement ring. After the third time, I lost it on him. I told him exactly where he can put the engagement ring. I mean... what did I have to lose at this point? As he said, I didn't deserve it anyway. Therefore, I found it

necessary to give him what he deserved and that was a piece of my mind. Boy oh boy did I blast off to him and gave him every choice word that I could think of. I had never been in this type of relationship. I had never been told that I didn't deserve an engagement ring. I had to make up in my mind that I wasn't going to be strung along any longer. I wanted so much better for myself. I wasn't quite sure how I
was going to accomplish it. It seemed like every time I tried to break away, here he would come with the sob story of how he missed me and that we should make up. I fell for it every time.

It wasn't until I had an emergency in 2006. Georgia Power mixed my bill up with three of my neighbors. In the neighborhood where we lived, they didn't charge us for our own individual usage. We were charge on an average of everyone's use in that neighborhood. Instead of averaging the bill, they added the bills of two other residents and then disconnected my service for non-payment on the date that I received the bill. I didn't get a chance to dispute it before the disconnection. By the time I was able to speak with them, the bill plus reconnection was $450. I asked Mr. Dressed Up in Lies to help me. He danced around the subject and played like he was going to send me the money. As a result, my children and I were in the dark. He wouldn't answer my calls nor would he text back. I had money that was pending but I didn't have access to it for 10 business days. I couldn't be with someone like this. How did I allow myself to be embraced in this foolishness? I called my uncle, who is my daddy's brother, to help me. He couldn't help right away, but he said that he would send the money the next morning.

I was able to pay the bill in enough time for my service to be restored the same day. I called Georgia Power to straighten the situation out. After dancing around with the customer service agent and the supervisor, they finally took care of it and I received a credit on my bill. Three days later, he called and said that he has the money. He said that he was going to wire it to me because he had been in meetings for the past several days. He apologized and asked for the location nearest me to send the money. Just to see if he was really going to do it, I gave him the information. He sent a reference code by text. I called Money Gram to see if there was any money for me. The lady said, "No sweetie. There isn't anything yet. Try back in about a half hour." I thought it was strange. So I took a chance and called back. Nothing.

I couldn't even get mad because I already knew. And of course, I didn't hear back from him until it was almost time for me to relocate back to California, which was February 2007. He called me when my baby girl was hospitalized and wanted to apologize. I couldn't understand how someone could be so cruel. It would have been more feasible for him to simply let me know that he didn't have it, or that he didn't want to do it rather than lie to me and leave me and my children in the dark. Ultimately, I blamed myself for being too fearful to speak my truth right then and there. Listening to his apology was like slow dancing with the devil and letting him whisper sweet nothings in my ear. Nothing that he was saying was true. Yet, I still couldn't break away. Emotionally, I couldn't let go, even though I wanted to. It was rough. No matter how bad or horrible he was to me, I felt an unspoken connection to him. I wanted to hate him, but I couldn't. He never raised his hands to hit me, but the emotional insidious deceit, treachery, falsifications & evil works that came forth from him were just as bad.

After my baby was released from the hospital, I began to pack and throw away things that I would not need to move back home. I moved out of my house and rented a hotel room for the final three weeks of residing in Georgia. I was returning home to help my gran'mommy. She was up in age and she was in the early stages of dementia. She told me that she was afraid to be alone. I left as soon as I was able to.

February 2007, I was going back to Cali. It was a long drive across the country. I was up for it. I had left the traditional school setting and enrolled in school online. I was in the process of completing my Bachelor's degree in Criminal Justice. Despite all that I was dealing with, I refused to quit. It was mandatory to press on to complete my education. I was a first generation college student. I was going to be the first one to complete college. Nonetheless, gran'mommy needed me and I was going to be there for her. Within two weeks I was employed. I enrolled my little girls in daycare and I was on the move. Life was good. The only time Mr. Dressed Up in Lies name was mentioned was when someone asked about him and we laughed at the lies that he told over the course of time.

24

He called me about three months after moving back. He came with his sob story once again. Ah ha… he suddenly had meetings that he was facilitating in the Northern California region. How convenient. I was determined that I was not going to fall prey to his tactics again. I was focused on my babies, which was a normal life task for me, working, and finishing school. I was single. I proceeded to go back to my church home at Cottonwood Christian Center in Los Alamitos, California. I was learning so much. I was growing in the Word of God. I was feeling whole, but I knew that there were still some things missing to complete the wholeness. Our conversations were hit and miss.

Thinking back about nine and a half years ago when my husband and I met. I had a dream and I could not quite put my finger on it but I saw Mr. Dressed Up in Lies. It was a DeJa'Vu moment. It just came to light why I could not put my finger on that dream. As I am writing my book or shall I say re-writing my manuscript for my book called the Day I Met My Boaz the dream suddenly appeared. I could not quite put my finger on it because it wasn't time. Initially I was almost done writing my manuscript and ready to submit it for editing. The dream came back to me that this one particular guy named Mr. Dressed Up in Lies appeared in that dream as someone who was trying to hold on to me and would not let me go. Just before I met My Boaz, Mr. Dressed Up in Lies wanted me to come and visit him. He wanted me to buy a plane ticket to visit him in Chicago or Atlanta. I told him that I will not purchase the ticket and that I will not buy anything to come and see him. If he wants to see me he will either buy the ticket to come to California or he would buy the tickets for me to come and see him.

Personally, I did not want to do either and because I knew that he would not do it I gave him those options. In essence I wasted time. What I am saying is do not allow yourself to be taken by someone else's lies and deceit and manipulative ways. This relationship was founded on lies. At the time he told me that he would purchase the tickets was in July 2010. The last time I spoke to him was in October 2010. He wanted to see me as he claimed. He said that it would take him some time to get thing settled because he was traveling for his job and that he will buy the tickets probably around the first part of spring of 2011. I hadn't heard anything from him since that time. When I finally did hear from him again, it was March 2011, and I was already engaged. I was deep into my relationship with my husband who at the time was my fiancé.

At the time, we were working on closing the gap to avoid all of the expensive travels of long distance relationship dating. I received a phone call from Mr. Dressed Up in Lies letting me know that he was ready to buy my tickets. I sat on the phone silent for a few minutes because I could not believe what I was hearing. So much had evolved in my life within a six-month time frame. One of the things that definitely changed was that I was no longer interested in relationships that were not growing and that never benefited me and only benefit at the other person. In other words, there were no mutual benefits. When I finally realized what was going on, simply because I literally forgot about the conversation six months earlier, I've read this dude from left to right and gave him the business all in one breath. I said, "While you were getting things together I got things together and I got them together with a man who is interested in me. He was so interested in me that he made sure that I went without nothing. He made sure that if I fell short he picked up all of the pieces. And, above all I am the ABSOLUTE center of his world. Have I ever been the Center of Your World? No I have always been lied to and told that you were coming to see me which you never have. To make matters better, we are together and engaged. You were going to call me back after all of these alleged meetings but you never did. I wasted three years of my life on foolishness with you." Actually instead of looking at it as wasted time I honestly see it as lessons learned. I concluded by saying, "Therefore, I will not be coming to see you nor will I be talking to you again; I am no longer interested." He asked me to hear him out before I hung up on him. I did. He said, "That really hurt me." I said, "I meant for it to." He said well I guess there's nothing more to say. I responded, "There isn't. Have a good life." I hung the phone up and I wanted nothing else from him. I felt liberated. I felt freed of the yoke of bondage that caused our souls to be tied. I also believe that this dream was held at bay because it was waiting to be entered into this book. I remember telling my husband after we had gotten together and right after this dream that he was my Boaz. I later told my husband about this dream.

I never expounded on the topic because I didn't know what it was about until today, May 3rd, 2020. The revelation solidified that I was soul tied to this guy and the soul tie needed to be broken and if I had continued communication with him I would not be where I am today.

What Was In It For Me?

I thought love was in it for me. I thought it would be a blissful ending that lead into the life that I wanted. So, what was in it for me was to see with my eyes and not with my heart. See the truth for what it really and truthfully is. When we fail to face the truth and accept it for what it is, we create within us false hope, relinquishing our power, and in the end, we can become depressed when things don't work out. Thus, feeling rejected and abandoned. What was in it for me? That also depends on how one perceives the chain of events. Granted, Mr. Dressed Up In Lies lied about everything from sunup to sundown. At the point of recognition of his lies, when do I take responsibility? That is just it. When I recognized it I should have made the move, but I didn't. Just like many women, I wanted to give him a chance to self-correct. I gave him too many chances. That is where the problem lies. I believe in giving an opportunity to self-correct. Since I learned better, I do better and now I have mastered it, if you fail to self-correct after a given number of times, it's a done deal. The number of times is very limited today, whereas, back then, I kept giving chance after chance.

LADIES... this is a huge mistake. Stop giving up your power. Stop losing the courage to let go. Stop moving in fear. We have all been there and done that on some level. At what point do you take responsibility for your actions? As a woman, if you continue to give of your power, lose courage, fail to overcome, and continue to move in fear, you will never attract the man that you want. I stress this because I was once there. Once you see that you have to level up and make changes that are beneficial for you, everyone, and everything else around you will benefit from it. When people began to fall off its typically because they can no longer use you, deceive you, manipulate you, as well as scheme and connive against you. You should want better for yourself. You have to know that you deserve better. The question still stands: What was in it for me?

As I reflect on this time in my life, I see what was in it for me was that I had to gain the power to cut people off who walked in this category. I had to gain the courage to let go and not fear the inevitable which was that he was not going to be a prominent and permanent part of my life. We were not

27

going to have a blissful ending. I also had to stop moving in fear and compromising myself. What I mean is I gave up things for me to make him happy and I was left holding his emotional baggage. Once I wised up and prayed about it I asked God to give him back everything that was in that bag because it did not belong to me. When someone drops their emotional, traumatic, rejected, and abandoned baggage off at your doorstep, on your couch, kitchen table, bedroom... if it doesn't rightfully belong to you, DO NOT be afraid to give it back. As a woman, I had to find and hold my power, build my courage, overcome the obstacles of rejection and abandonment, and walk as a fearless, EMPOWERED giant as I took a stand for what I wanted. If you know the type of man you want, go to Habakkuk 2:2-4 and follow directions. It doesn't get any plainer than that. This is what was in it for me. I had to own it. I had to be honest with myself. I had to stop believing his lies and see it for what it really was. I did not have the right to be angry with him because he was acting accordingly. Once I realized that our seasons didn't sync I should have closed it off. But I didn't. That does not give him a pass to do all that he did and it does not excuse him for his behavior. However, I cannot be responsible for him. I own my responsibility to myself in this situation.

REGRETS? NONE! I walked away like the woman I am with my head held high. I made peace with this situation and I gracefully moved on.

How Did I Walk Away?

I stopped looking through the looking-glass and faced the truth that Mr. Dressed Up in Lies was just that. He presented himself in such a way that I was attracted to him. He was everything that I thought that I wanted. In actuality, he was all of the hell that I felt about myself. I had daddy issues. I longed for the love of my father (definitely not in a romantic way). However, my issues stemmed from having no blueprint. I didn't know much about how to be in a successful relationship. It was always something going on. It was always something to add to my stress level.

Initially, I had a low sense of my end of the relationship. It is always easy to blame the other person. It takes two to tango. Therefore, I know that I had to own my end of the relationship. The most difficult part is admitting. I had to be honest with myself. I had to weigh the pros and cons of WWIIFM –

what was in it for me. I couldn't take anything positive away from this relationship.

God blessed me with two sisters from other mothers and other misters. They are my unbiological sisters. They poured into me heavily. They gave me information that will forever be embedded in my mind. I had to learn. I was hungry for change.

I had to break the soul ties. I remember doing this before My Boaz and I became engaged.

CHAPTER THREE

Mr. Totally Ambivalent

I met Mr. Totally ambivalent after moving back to California in Spring of 2007. He was tall and very handsome. He was a little slender but had a nice physique. His tone of voice was deep and talked all corporate America'ish. It all started one evening at the donut shop in Compton right in the center of town. I was purchasing some doughnuts and chocolate milk, which is my all-time favorite. He struck up a conversation with me. Me being the friendly person that I am I talked back. I was intrigued by the initial conversation. It was nothing out of the ordinary or nothing inappropriate, just mutual conversation. I sat down to eat my donuts and he asked if he could sit with me. I still didn't think anything of it. As I proceeded to drink my chocolate milk and eat my donuts he asked me if he could keep in touch with me. He asked for my phone number. I was a little hesitant. I fell for the deep voice. I eventually said yes. Yes to the date and yes to giving him my phone number. He called later that evening to let me know that he wanted to keep his word and that he was excited about taking me on a date. We were on the phone for roughly 20 minutes. I let him know that I had to get my girls prepared for the next day and that I will talk to him later.

Before I went to bed he called me again. He expressed just how much he really wanted to get to know me in his level of excitement for wanting to take me out. Now I had one eyebrow raised with skepticism because your level of excitement is excessively high for someone you just met, which was my thought. He called me the next day. This time, we talked for roughly two hours getting to know each other and our likes and dislikes. We talked about our children as well as the type of careers that we were in. Eventually, we talked about our first date in where we should go. He had it all planned out.

He suggested Mastro's Steakhouse. He was definitely on point with my food palate.

The day was finally here. I hit the gym first thing that morning. I went home, showered, and headed to the nail salon to get my nails done and get a pedicure. It was at that moment that I received a phone call confirming that we were still on for the evening. I expressed my excitement and told him yes I was excited to go out with him and I look forward to spending a nice evening. He asked me if I liked jazz. Smooth jazz is definitely one of my favorite genres. You can mix Sade as well as Boney James and come up with an elixir to calm the soul. I went to a boutique in Lakewood right off of the 91 freeway at Artesia. I bought me an outfit for the evening and some new shoes. I knew that I would steal the evening. Dinner and smooth jazz were right up my alley. He didn't say where we would go to listen to smooth jazz. But I was up for it. My girls were taken care of for the evening. I went to take my shower and laid my clothes out on my bed. As I was preparing to beat my face, my phone rang. Undoubtedly, it was him. He said that he had to go to the hospital to see about his son. His son fell and hit his head and had a seizure. I let him know that I totally understood and for him to go ahead and take care of his baby and to let me know that his baby is okay. He was two years old at the time and more than likely needed his mommy and his daddy by his side. I totally understood. In the process my dad's wife and his stepdaughter kept calling me to see how I was doing, if I was excited, and what my plans were for the evening. I let them know that he had to cancel because he had to go to the hospital to see about his baby boy. I had never dealt with anything like this so it was unusual for me to sit and wait for this man to call me back. He did call and tell me that they were waiting for a CT scan and they were waiting for some other test to come back. I told him that I understood and that I will keep his baby in prayer. As a mother my heart went out to him and the mother of this baby as well as the baby. I put my T-shirt on and some lounging pants. I laid down to relax and listen to some smooth jazz. Eventually, I dozed off. My Dad's wife called me and asked if I was depressed. I explained to her that I had fallen asleep listening to some smooth jazz. She insisted that I was falling into a depression. I told her that I could not fall into a depression behind someone I did not know nor had a relationship with. I did express that I was concerned because of his baby. My maternal instinct felt sorrowful for them as parents. Outside of that I was not depressed. She kept asking me the same question redundantly as if I did not understand what she was asking. I explained to her that I am not DEPRESSED. Finally, we got off the phone. Her daughter called me the next day and said, "Mamma said that you was depressed and that I should talk to you. What's going on?" I explained what happen to his son and I got comfortable in my t shirt and lounge pants and eventually, fell asleep listening to smooth jazz. She said, "Mamma said you is depressed. If you having trouble keeping a man I can tell you what to do to keep a man." By now my blood is boiling. "If I tell you that I am not depressed take my word for it," I explained to her loud and clear, "I am not depressed." I don't know this man to be depressed about anything that he has going on.

As a mother, I understood the emotional pain that he and this child's mother may have felt with their child having to go into the hospital. Further, there isn't anything they you personally can teach me about keeping a man. The argument was on. She said, "I've been with my boyfriend 10 years." I responded, "Yay you! That right there is the one reason that you can never tell me how to keep a man. YOU! After the situations I've dealt with I will never be someone's girlfriend longer than two years without having nuptials." While I loved her boyfriend, thought of him as family, and thought he was the perfect match for her, I still would not agree to be a girlfriend for that long. That is what worked for them and I never judged her by it until she came for me. I told her there are things in your relationship that I would never go for in mines. "So, watch who you are saying you can teach how to keep a man because what works for you ABSOLUTELY DOES NOT work for me," I said. This conversation would have gone a lot different if she would have said something along the lines of "let me take you out," "let's go and have some ice cream," or, "let's go to a movie to take your mind off things and if you feel like talking about something let's talk and if you don't I respect that." She insisted that she could teach me how to keep a man.

The dynamics of their relationship is that they both were living at home with their mothers. I am not sure about him but I know she had never lived on her own at that point. There is absolutely nothing you can teach me about keeping a man, because a part of my idea of a man is someone who is able to manage his own place and his own money outside of his parents. He may have been with his mom for a very good reason. I never asked because it wasn't my business. I know what I needed. This is not to put down a man

32

who lives at home with his mother or his mother and father or his father or whoever he lives with who takes care of the majority of the home. Her boyfriend was very good to her. However, the only thing that she could teach me out of that situation was as far as she knew and that was the measure of their relationship. I wanted something totally different. She didn't approach me with principles of a relationship. She didn't approach me to empower me. She didn't approach me to help me learn anything. She approached me and such a way that it was a put down as it always had been. The tone of her voice and the words that she used let me know that she felt on top of the world because she had all these years in this relationship with this gentleman. One thing I learned is that you have to be careful how you approach someone and how you speak on their situation because you never know if and when that can be you. The next day Mr. Totally Ambivalent called me and gave me an update about his baby boy. He was in no way obligated to tell me any of this business. I thanked him for keeping me in the loop. I let him know that I was happy that his son came out on top of his situation. He asked me if I still wanted to go on the date because there was another location that we could go to for some smooth jazz after. I said yes again. As the evening approached I took my clothes out again. I was preparing to do my make up again. I felt like I should call him to confirm. So I did. He gave me an excuse and said that he was too tired from being at the hospital from the night before. He asked me can we make it another night. I was very apprehensive at this point. I told him to call me whenever he was ready and if I am available at that time, I would be happy to go out. About a week went by and he finally called me. He asked me for another date. I asked if he is sure that he wants to go out with me. It seemed as though I was on this hamster wheel with him. He promised that he was going to be there. He stated that he would come and pick me up and that we would have a wonderful night on the town. While this was ideal, I wasn't so trusting. I explained to him that I could just meet him wherever he wanted to meet. He said that he didn't mind. He then asked if I would mind driving him. I said, "Yes I do." You take your car and I will take mine. He then asked me if I would mind having a night in. I said yes I do mind having a night in. My clothes were ready. I had to slip into them. I didn't even beat my face because I was not sure about this evening.

Suddenly he got another call and had to go. I thought to myself this is not going anywhere. He promised that he was going to call me back. I asked him straight out, "Are you a street pharmacist?" He assured me that he wasn't. I let him know that his behavior was so erratic and ambivalent. He assured me that everything was on point and that he was going to call me back. It was at 4 o'clock in the morning when my phone rang. I thought to myself how I could give him every choice word in the urban dictionary. I also thought this is a waste of time. I was prepared to cut this off and move on. I decided not to answer my phone. He kept calling. I put the phone in the drawer and turned over. I went back to sleep. A few weeks went by. Here he comes again. He called me to explain. I let him know that YOU do not have permission to call me at 4:00 a.m. We do not have children together, we are not in a relationship, and that we probably never will be at this rate. The only places open at that hour is 7/11 and a pair of legs. Mine was closed and closed tightly. He pleaded with me to hear him out. I listened. It was nothing that really made me interested. He asked me if I would give him one last chance to prove himself. RELUCTANTLY, I agreed. He promised to follow through. Shaking my head at myself, I went with it. It was Friday after work. I was on my way to the gym in Compton. I had a physical fitness exam coming up for the job at Los Angeles County Probation Department.

After the gym, I showered and went to Jamba Juice in Gardena for a smoothie. I watched a little bit of television while chopping it up with one of my favorite girls. As the nightfall grew darker, my eyes got heavier. Finally, I called it a night. When I awakened, I decided to choose a different outfit and buy another pair of shoes for our date. Shoes are my fetish. I went to the nail salon again for a fill and a new pedicure. I wasn't going to call him. I thought positive and gave him the benefit of the doubt. By the time my nail lady was polishing my nails, he called me. His son had to go back to the hospital Friday night. He was doing fine. However, his mother was going out and she didn't have a babysitter. He volunteered. I was angry. By now, I am rolling my eyes in my head and hoping that he can feel the shade thrown at him in my conversation. He took it as though I didn't want him to be around his son. As a woman who barely had her father, that is not something that I would ever consider telling a man. Further, I was angry because I kept allowing this to go on. In fact, we danced around this for about
two years off and on. It was the same redundant pattern of he wanted to take me out, then his son had a seizure, his son's mom – which is also his ex-wife – needed him to babysit every time we had something scheduled. I was tired. I couldn't dance to this beat any longer.

Soon, I ended this non-relationship situationship, so I thought. He felt the need to keep calling me. One day I answered. I was VERY rude. He said, "I

34

need someone to talk to." I said, "Call your ex-wife. Y'all seem to vibe off of each other's drama." He responded, "Ouch... I probably deserved that. Do you have some time? I just need someone to talk to." RELUCTANTLY, I asked, "What do you want?" He said, "My ex-wife is in the hospital. I am hoping that she is alright. She had some bleeding coming from her rectum." THAT WAS IT! I LITERALLY LOST IT. I said, "I am not sure why you think that I should or would care. I don't want to know this woman's business. I don't wish her no ill. But I don't care. Don't call me anymore.!" I slammed the phone down. I started to cry. It was one of those cries where you want to put hands on someone but you are nowhere near them to reach out and touch. Yeah... one of those cries. I was infuriated. I couldn't quite understand the meaning of all this. Soon, the feelings of abandonment, rejection and "he's just not that into you" began to set in." After dealing with this, my thought of celibacy took over. The idea of chilling out and refocusing looked better and better. I chose celibacy with a purpose. Even though he would still call me from time to time, I still kept it short and sweet and moved on with my life. I pressed into my education. I pressed into where I needed to be with the Lord. I hung out with some cousins and friends occasionally and did things that would be beneficial for me.

It is now the beginning of 2008, approximately one year later. Mr. Totally Dressed in Lies called. He wanted to do the long distance thing, since my move to California wasn't intended to be permanent. He claimed to want to pursue marriage. He claimed that he wanted to see me. What's worse is that he knew that this is what I wanted. The question still remained, "Is he someone who I could have this with?" Despite all of the previous challenges that I went through with him, I did consider it. I had some business to square away in Georgia so I thought it might be okay to go and see him while I am handling my business. He offered to rent my car so that I could get around. Although I didn't need him to, I agreed.

Upon my arrival to Atlanta, he picked me up and we went to his place. I reserved a hotel because I didn't trust him. I didn't want to get caught up in the midst of any of his unknowns. We went to his apartment and I thought all hell had broken loose. It was EXTREMELY messy. The dishes were piled up to the ceiling. It was awful. I thought that he had lost his mind. I wanted to go to my hotel room and never return to that place again. He had the nerve to ask if I would clean it up. I promise... some of the foulest words known to mankind were running through my mind. I quickly said,

"NIGGA, I AM NOT THE MAID AND I AM NOT YOUR MAID.
You tried my boogie!"

I was over this. There was no way that he could woo me with marriage or anything else at this point. I asked for my rental so that I can leave to take care of my business. He asked me to sit tight so that he can run a few errands. I looked around and seen his bank statements. They were all in the open. Everything was in the red. Five different accounts all in the red. They were thousands of dollars in the red. I knew then that it was a wrap. It started to make sense. This is why he always lied about everything and told the truth about nothing when it pertained to money. He even asked for my children's social security numbers to allegedly make them his beneficiaries on his life insurance. Chile-boo... I answered him like I was Sophia in the Color Purple, "HELL NAW!" I tooted my face up proudly just like she did when the mayor's wife asked her to be the maid. There was no way. God knew that I had to see it. I needed to be released from this. He gave me the money for my rental and I left. I think I laughed harder than I was mad.

After arriving back in Cali, I proceeded on my regiment to celibacy. I was proud of myself for not giving in to Mr. Dressed Up In Lies. No sex. No touchy-feely. NOTHING. Soon, I felt like this was a game of tag because Mr. Totally Ambivalent wanted to communicate about US. No matter how bad I thought I wanted this with him, I couldn't bring myself to say yes. There were too many unknown variables and too many times that I was left hanging. This was absolutely the tone that he was setting for the future. He and Mr. Dressed Up In Lies seemed to be calling me often and sometimes, simultaneously. I continued to keep my focus. Passing every exam for Los Angeles County Probation
Department was my goal. I took the initial exam. I needed to pass with 90%. I made 96%. After taking the exam, the proctor announced that anyone who passed with 95% or higher was on their way to an interview. Everyone else would be notified at a later date. After my interview, I wanted to celebrate. My cousins and I went to Red Robin at the South Bay Galleria in Redondo Beach. We had a good time. We laughed and caught up on these dudes who kept playing tag. Although they didn't know each other, nor did they know of the other, it seemed like they knew the right time to hit me up. I thank God for His strength. I was still weak, but I was stronger than I was after I broke things off with Mr. Dressed Up In Lies and Mr. Totally Ambivalent. I am literally applauding myself for standing my ground. I continued on my daily regimen. I went to work, hit the gym, went to bible

study, church on Sundays and hung out with my same circle when we were able to. REPEAT.

My focus game was strong. I passed all of my exams for the job of a Detention Services Officer. I was offered the job in November 2008. I went through the training and passed my physical training exam. I graduated out of the Juvenile Correctional Officer Core Training and was placed at my facility in January 2009. I maintained my regiment. Still celibate, I continued to focus until February of that same year. Mr. Totally Ambivalent called once again. He said that he wanted to spend Valentine's Day with me and then asked me to be his lady. We had a long conversation about his pattern and how his promises to take me out made me feel uncomfortable. He promised that he changed. At the end of the conversation, I said yes. My dad's wife called me to have a quick chat. I told her what was going on with Mr. Totally Ambivalent. I expressed how I was feeling about the situation. Not long after I said how I was feeling, trying to maintain positivity and not think ill of the situation because of how things were in the past, she said, "God will never bless you with a good man. You don't even know what a good man looks like." I was devastated. What's worse, Mr. Totally Ambivalent left me hanging on Valentine's Day. That's right, I spent it alone. Now, I was depressed. I was angry. This man came with much baggage. The inevitable question came up when I finally spoke to him again. I asked, "Are you married?" He said, "No I am not married." I asked, "Are you seeing someone else?" He responded, "No I am not." "Then what is it?" He didn't have an answer. I was very emotional. I let him know that I need answers. I couldn't keep going on like that. I made a decision to let it go at this point.

Principles to Avoid Ambivalence

1.   Know YOURESELF: The pinnacle of self-esteem ultimately culminates in self-realization. At some point, I realized that I needed to refocus on things that were beneficial to my future. However, I still allowed myself to get lost in some points of the moment with him.

2.   Change your way of thinking to change your life: Acknowledge where you are and how you got there. Own your part of the situation. Count cost of everything – weighing pros and cons. Make changes that heal.

3.   Empower yourself: Do NOT give your power away. Find ways to encourage yourself. Get around people who will lift your morale. Most of all, READ THE WARNING SIGNS when they are staring you in the face.

Stand confidently and boldly in your courage, set out to overcome and move fearlessly.

4.	Set clear and concise boundaries: Establishing clear boundaries will definitely help you to know when to cut a situation off. If I had known then what I know now, this non-relationship situationship would never have earned two years of my time.

5.	Demand your respect: You can demand your respect without saying a word. Your presence should be bold enough to command the atmosphere.

a.	Come into the current atmosphere
b.	Stand with confidence and boldness
c.	Maintain a meek spirit
d.	DO NOT be afraid to walk away from a situationship because it isn't meeting the needs of the season that you're in
e.	Speak with the same confidence and boldness and DO NOT dance around with your answers and responses
f.	Don't be mean, but mean what you say and don't be swayed by what you see and hear
g.	If you have to walk away, do so with that same boldness and confidence, letting the other person know that "Ain't nobody got time fa dat," in my Sweet Brown voice – do this without opening your mouth.

What Was In It For Me?

The easy and obvious answer would be to say that there was nothing in it for me in this situation. I believe that I was hopin', and a wishin', and a prayin' that he would come through. Strangely, his ways resembled that of my dad in many aspects. Even though a lot of the hell, low self-esteem, feelings of worthlessness and fear of rejection was in me, I still attracted guys who were like my dad on some level. When my dad was on his deathbed he told me just how much he lied to me. He told me that he knew I needed things; he refused to make it happen for me. He told me that he didn't have a reason. This was devastating news for me. What's worse is he delivered this news to me Christmas of 2005. This was a time that is supposed to be about celebrating the birth of our Savior. Here I am bawling at the eyes in disbelief, grief, and anger. I honestly believe I allowed myself to be taken by Mr. Totally Ambivalent because I saw certain characteristics of my dad.

Typically, girls who grow into women tend to attract men who is/was like their fathers. There were certain things about him that drew me in. I know it might sound cheesy but it's the truth. Regardless of the fact the time came for me to woman up and face the reality that this was not going anywhere. What was in it for me was to get out of my head and get unstuck. He was a tad bit better than Mr. Dressed Up In Lies because he lived close by. As far as how he treated me, his lies, manipulation, and deceit, was all the same. I had to reflect what happened with Mr. Dressed Up In Lies. I repeated the same cycle. Therefore, I had to go back to God and pray and ask him to take this baggage and give it back to him. Repeating these cycles is not a game and it is not fun. Until you learn to break generational curses, you will keep repeating cycles in not understand what is going on. I went back to the drawing board and started over. What was in it for me is that I had to forgive myself or repeating this same cycle as well as find the courage to build on once again, overcome, gain empowerment, and move on fearlessly.

What was in it for me was that I had to acknowledge my anger with my dad. I had to acknowledge the abandonment and rejection that I felt. I had to allow myself to feel the pain deep within my heart. This is an extremely agonizing and emotional segment, but it is worth it because it started the process to getting free. I knew that I still had work to do. However, with every step, I moved closer to the freedom that I sought.

DISAPPOINTMENTS? MANY! I was not going to stop trying to get unstuck. My determination was eminent healing. Although I did move on gracefully, I realized that this was his character. I didn't have to make his proclivities mine. Therefore, I chose to level-up and make time for me. This was to be fulfilled with a purpose and to bring my level of self-worth up. Do your work. You won't regret it.

CHAPTER FOUR

Mr. Love Pistol

In late September 2009, I started dating a man who I thought would be cool. In the beginning we had fun. We both had four children each, three girls and one boy, EACH! In my mind I always knew that it was a lot of children. I came from a family where I have five brothers, one biological sister and one stepsister. This is on my dad's side. On my mother's side, I have three brothers. He only had one sibling who was his older brother. There were many times I wondered if anything would become of our relationship. I will never forget the night that he said, "If anything ever happens to us, don't ever let anyone tell you that you are not an AWESOME woman." I thought nothing of it. I said, "Okay." I proceeded on. I thought about it from time to time, but never inquired about it. We spent Halloween together because his children went to Knott's Scary Farm. It was a cool night, and we got to know one another a little better. We found out we liked a lot of the same foods and places. He had a job and his own place. He also had his own vehicle. He had his own relationship with the Lord. It was a breath of fresh air.

After hanging out a few times and having many conversations on the phone, he asked me to be his lady. I said yes. He lived in Los Angeles, California. I lived in Corona Hills, California. His house wasn't the best, but it was his. I lived in some luxury townhome apartments off of the 91 Freeway and McKinley Street. I started spending a lot of time at his house because of the time that he got off work. I was off work on an injury. So I had nothing but time. I wanted to spend some of my time with him. I saw things that was lacking in his place, such as tissue, paper towels, food, etc. I would purchase these things because I was there, and my children were with me. We planned to spin our holidays

together that year. As much as I was trying to make things work between us, it somehow seemed to have fissures running through everything. Amid all of this, I was enrolled in school to complete my Master's degree in Forensic Psychology. He enrolled to complete his Bachelor's degree in something. I believe that it had something to do with CAD. He lost me when he kept hinting that he needed a co-signer for his student loans. I ignored him. He kept saying that he needed a co-signer. Finally, he asked, "Can you please cosign for my student loan?" With the swiftness, my head spent around like the exorcist and my eyes rolled quickly, I said, "NO! My name goes on nothing for no one unless it is my husband. Sorry. Won't be me!" My thoughts continued on to the holiday season.

Thanksgiving was okay. I cooked at his place. He took me to meet his mother afterwards. She seemed to be cool and gave me kudos as his lady. She told him I was a keeper. Suddenly, the fissures mended themselves. We talked about having a life together someday. We talked about plans for our children. I developed my relationship with them. His son was the strangest kid. However, the talk of having a serious future was on the table. He revealed to me he was called to preach the Word of God. He asked, "Can you handle the fact that I will be preaching the Word of God?" What woman can't handle that? I answered, "Of course I can handle that. It's the other stuff that will be a problem." He never questioned the other stuff. I never elaborated. It was as if he already knew what I was talking about.

Soon, it would be Christmas. We made plans to spend Christmas at my place since we spent Thanksgiving at his place. My son came home from Georgia to visit because his birthday is December 23rd. This time in this year was so chaotic. My mother was driving one of my cars and told me she no longer needed my car because she was getting one of her own. A friend of mine needed a vehicle, so I told her about the one that my mother no longer needed. Prior to getting the car back from my mother, she was complaining about having to put a new battery in it and change the tires. You have been driving it. Therefore, that is the least that you can do, especially since I was still paying the loan and insurance on it. The night of my son's kick back, which was on his birthday, my friend, her fiancé, their children, and a few other friends came over. My mother pulled up and acted a complete fool in the parking lot of my luxury apartment complex. The boyfriend pulled up and all of my guests were outside with me watching my mother perform as usual when things wouldn't go her way. She kept saying that she wanted her battery out of THAT car before my friend took possession of it. It was after 9:00 pm on the west coast. There was no way that anyone would remove a battery in my complex. That was against the policies of my lease and I wasn't taking any chances. Eventually, I told my friend and her fiancé to leave. If she didn't leave, my mother would have continued to carry on foolishly.

Boyfriend stood there still. He looked at me and then shook his head and walked in my townhome. My friends stood around in silence. All I could do is apologize. I was embarrassed, and I didn't offer an apology for her behavior. The night ended with silence roaming the air. I didn't know what to say. I rolled over and went to sleep.

It was Christmas eve. The boyfriend woke me up and let me know that he was leaving for work and that he would see me later on in the evening. I prepared my grocery list for some last-minute shopping. I had already finished my Christmas shopping. I hadn't planned on leaving my house on Christmas day. My plan was to cook on Christmas morning and relax for the rest of the day. We stayed up playing board games and laughing and enjoying the evening. After everyone had gone to bed, I prepped some of my food, then I went to bed. His mother called around noon on Christmas day. She wanted us to go over to his brother's fiancé's home in Rancho Cucamonga, California. I was reluctant because I had already had plans. He could go, but I wanted to stay home. She called and called and called. She wanted us to be there, and she wanted us there at a certain time. We discussed none of this with me prior to her phone call. Had they had discussed it with me prior to Christmas day, I probably would have visited willingly. He tried to explain to her I was cooking my food, but that we were coming. She wanted me to stop what I was doing and go right then. Unfortunately for her, that is not how it works in my world. I insisted that he goes to be with his family and that I will stay home and finish cooking my food. He insisted that I go with him. This became an argument. Finally, he asked, "Will you please go with me to my brother's for Christmas dinner?"

I stared at him like the flushed face emoji.

I finally agreed. I showered, got dressed, and we left. We arrived a little after 5:00 pm. His mother was livid. She talked trash as we were walking through the door. My second daughter and my Babygirl wanted some macaroni and some turkey. She asked me if she could fix them something to eat. I gave her the go ahead (after she washed her hands). His mother said, "If you don't get up and fix their plates, I will drop kick you in your face!" IMMEDIATELY, I said, "HA! Yeah okay." They ruined Christmas 2009. My mood was very unstable for the rest of the evening while we were there. This is one of the main reasons I don't enjoy going places when I am not driving my vehicle so that I can leave when I am ready. I sat there for four dreadful hours. A friend texted me to send holiday wishes. She asked how my day was going. When I told her everything that was going on she couldn't believe it. I asked her to keep texting me to kill time. She agreed. She knew that I was angry. His mother assumed that I was texting him. His mother said, "He ain't leaving no time soon because he is up there with his brother and they are on the video game and the DJ Equipment." I replied, "SO." I continued to text my friend. The rest of the party had nothing to say to me and left me alienated at the dinner table while they were in another room laughing and having a good time. I was totally excluded.

Finally, he came downstairs and asked me if I was ready. I jumped up and said, "Let's go y'all. It's been a night." I walked out the door and said nothing to no one. Me and my children were in the car waiting. When he got in the car, he asked, "What happened?" I gave him the rundown and told him I am good. I never want to do anything with his family again. His children? Yes. His mother and brother? NOPE. Approximately four days went by before he spoke to his mother again. I explained to him if he is going to be upset with his mother, then be upset with her. He was not obligated to avoid speaking with her because of me. When he finally spoke to her, she planted the seed of manipulation in his ear. She kept telling him I was coming between them. I had no clue what she was talking about, especially since I never told him he couldn't see his mother and family. That is not my place, nor is it my business. Soon, the fissures showed up again, and the relationship became rocky. My birthday would soon be approaching. I feared spending it alone. He seemed to not care for our relationship anymore.

We spent a few days apart. He didn't call me, and I didn't call him. When he finally called, he said that he had been looking for an apartment because he was tired of living in the old raggedy house in Los Angeles. He relocated to Orange County. He moved near the area where I spent most of my latter years of high school. I was very familiar with the area. He told me he would definitely take me out for my birthday. He asked me what I wanted to do. I wanted to spend a weekend in San Diego. Instead of doing what I wanted to do, he took me to the Long Beach Aquarium, and we did a harbor cruise. We ate dinner at Medieval Times. The money he spent could have definitely gone towards the trip to San Diego. We didn't have to go on my birthday just as long as it was in the same month. I appreciated what he did, but it wasn't what I wanted for my special day. He gave me a promise ring. It was nice, but still wasn't what I wanted.

We were on the outs when Valentine's day came around. There again, I thought things would be special. Instead, I was alone. We were on again and off again. The next time that we were on again, I remember walking into his apartment and standing in the living room. It was as though my feet couldn't move. He asked, "What's wrong with my sweet love?" I replied, "I don't belong here anymore." I knew something was off, but I couldn't put my finger on it. He took my bag off my shoulder and put it in the room. I literally followed my bag and thought I should leave. I went against the grain and stayed, regardless of how I felt. I felt uncomfortable and no matter what I did, I just couldn't shake the feeling. I left the next day to take care of some business. I told him I would see him later. Two days went by. He called me to ask if I was coming over because he wanted to see me. Initially, I told him I would stay home. He was convincing, plus I wanted to see him too. When I arrived at his apartment again, I had the same feeling. He knew what I would say. I didn't belong there. He took my bag again and told me he made dinner. I blatantly ignored what I was feeling. I tried to make it go away. After I ate, I took a shower and went to sit on the bed. I noticed that the sheets had been changed. I couldn't understand why the sheets had been changed if we hadn't been intimate when I was there the last time. Everything just seemed off.

The next day, I went to my hair appointment with my two youngest daughters. I took his youngest daughter. She always looked pitiful and never had her hair done. I asked him if it was okay to get her hair done. I didn't know her mother, and she wasn't my child, even though she would call me mommy. He gave me the go ahead to get her hair washed and pressed. Our hair was always immaculate when leaving the salon. When he saw us, he spoke, but he complimented his daughter and said nothing to my two daughters, despite all three girls having the same hairstyle. All three of the girls, his youngest daughter and my two daughters had really long

44

hair. I went off on him. Not only did you not have to pay for her hair, but you could have at least complimented all of them together and gave your daughter more compliments when my daughters weren't around. This turned into an argument. In the interim, my sister called me, and we started shooting the breeze. I told her what happened. She got so angry with me for doing things for him. She would ask, "What was he doing before you came along?" Her logic was that if he and her mother didn't get that child's hair done, then I shouldn't have bothered. My logic was that I didn't want her to feel left out. It boosted her confidence and made her feel pretty.

Over the next couple of months, the cycle repeated until his birthday came around. It was the beginning of April 2010. The girls and I got our hair done and we all left to San Clemente and had a fabulous time. All of the kids were together. I remember letting him hold my camera and he asked me to take some pictures of him. He took some of me too. But, he then asked me to take more pictures of him. The weekend came to an end. We went back to his apartment. He had been on my mini laptop and downloaded the pictures from the weekend on there. In the midst of him downloading, his friend stopped by. It was late in the evening. Everyone had taken their shower. I fell asleep. When I awakened, he had already left for work. Me and my daughters were packing to go home. His oldest daughter wanted to come with us. I grabbed my mini laptop and we left. When I arrived home, I dropped all of my laundry in the washing machine since it was in the garage. I went upstairs to my bedroom, showered, and opened the laptop. After opening it, I seen his emails. The first conversation was with a woman who he was planning on marrying, according to the email. I read the whole thread. She asked him about me. In his response, he told her that I was nobody to him and that all he wanted was her.

I called him. Suddenly, my calls were being avoided. So I called and called and called. I kept getting swerved to the voicemail. Later in the evening, he finally answered. All of a sudden, he can't talk. He said, "I will call you back." I kindly got in my car and showed up at his apartment. Talk about a surprise... he was about to have sex with an older woman for a flatscreen television. I asked the woman if she was the woman in the email. She confirmed that she wasn't and had no clue who I was talking about. Not that it matters, but I lost it. I had all of these flashbacks to the things that he said to me. It all made sense. I just asked for my things and then I would leave. The lady wanted me to leave. I called her some really unkind names and told her not to say a word to me. He refused to give me my belongings and told me that I gave him everything. He said, "These are gifts. You ain't getting nothing back!" The one thing that I clearly recalled in this moment was that he said, "If anything ever happens to us, don't ever let anyone tell you that you are not an AWESOME woman." It all came back to me. Out of my rage, I said, "GIVE ME MY THINGS OR I AM GOING TO TEAR YOU AND YOUR PLACE UP!" This was the ultimate confirmation that this relationship was over.

What got me in trouble is that I was an officer. The police told me that I should have known better. They didn't arrest me. My sister came to pick me up. She took me home. I was so angry. I couldn't see straight. She wanted to get her goons after him. I told her that even though I was angry enough to spit fire on him, he wasn't worth it. The next day, I was informed that a warrant had been issued for my arrest. I called an attorney and retained his services. He went to court and had the warrant pulled. He worked the case in my favor. He let the ex know that I would win against him because I have all of the receipts for all of the things that he refused to give me. He advised him that he would get jail time if he pressed the issue to have me press charges against him. He let him know that what he did is called theft by deception, theft by taking and the value of the items would get him some significant jail time. Suddenly, the charges all went away.

I spent days being angry. I was more angry at myself. I remember the feelings that I had when I should have left. I felt it. I did not belong there. I beat myself up emotionally. I became extremely angry at both of my parents. The mother would call me. I didn't want to talk to her. She irritated me from my skin to my inner-being. She had the nerve to say, "You act like you don't want to talk to me." My response was, "What gave it away?" I was angry with her because she has never been there and this was a situation that I couldn't trust her with. She can't hold water and I couldn't trust her with my pain. I had to figure out how to deal with this. My first step was repentance. I had to go to God and humble myself and repent. I asked Him for forgiveness. I knew that I was wrong. I knew that I should have left the first time that I felt like I didn't belong there. I cried out for God to show me what I need to do to change. I could not go on like this. I was tired of dating and not getting any further than where I was. I was stuck. It was an awful place to be.

Warning Signs

There were several warning signs that I did not pay attention to. Although I saw the signs, I didn't act on them. It was more than an instinct. It was the Holy Spirit. There were so many things that he said and things that happened that should have led to the demise of this relationship a lot sooner than it did. Even though I was angry about this breakup, I had to own my part. I had to accept the responsibility for knowing that I felt out of place and I stayed. It was a spirit of heaviness that came over me. I chose to stick it out. I hoped, wished, and prayed. Regardless, it was over and I wasn't looking back. His oldest daughter gave me that final push to confirm the whole reality. She said, "My daddy will be back. He always circulates his women in and out." I said, "Your daddy won't ever have that chance again with me. As God is my witness, he will never have this opportunity again by the grace of God." I meant that and I stuck to it. Proverbs 11:14 (CEB) Without guidance, a people will fall, but there is victory with many counselors. I sought counsel. I went to someone who knew nothing about me and had nothing to gain or lose by telling me the truth. I wanted the pure unadulterated truth on what I needed to do. The first thing that was said to me was that I don't pay attention to the warning signs.

There my face was with that blank look.

She gave me some homework and set me an appointment to see her the following week. I did the homework and returned for my appointment. As time went on, I saw my growth. I was on my pursuit
for eminent change and healing. It was imperative. I didn't want to see myself in this situation again. I pounded the pavement making power moves for healing. I refused to allow depression and anxiety to overtake me and to be my portion.

What Was In It For Me?

EVERYTHING was in it for me. ENOUGH was E FREAKING NUFF already. This was it. I'd had it. Never before have I witnessed anything like this in my life. Here I was, yet again. Another FAILED relationship. So now, the common denominator was me FOR SURE. There is no way that I was going to continue my life on this path. What was in it for me?
&EMINENT CHANGE. CHOOSING TO HEAL.
&CHOOSING TO BE AND STAY EMPOWERED.

&CHOOSING TO STAND COURAGEOUSLY

&WHEN EVERYTHING IS FAILING AND
&FALLING APART RIGHT BEFORE MY EYES.

&CHOOSING TO OVERCOME.
&CHOOSING NOT TO WALK IN FEAR.

I dug deep. I knew, even if I never met my Boaz, I had to heal. My anger against my dad grew deeper and deeper. I was so angry with him that in the midst of a breakdown, I cried out to God about the devastating effects of where he and my mother dropped me off at Failure Parkplace. WHY? WHY LORD? Why would they have me only to leave me to the wolves. I couldn't figure it out. What was my purpose? Who am I supposed to be? God's woman? What did she look like? Surely, she didn't look like me. The unbiological sister who picked me up during the chaos with Mr. Love Pistol, hounded me to understand the beauty within me. She would tell me that it would break her heart to see me going through such difficult situations. She always told me that my heart is so big but that I never give anything to myself.

What was in it for me? I listened endlessly to Christian radio. When I heard scenarios that were similar to mine, I thought about the Holy Spirit and how I seemed to be at the right place at the right time. The

advice was given by Christian counselors. They gave the pure, unadulterated truth to their callers. I took the advice for myself when it was appropriate, which seemed to be often. I studied scriptures and made sure to call out anything that was plaguing me. If I didn't know the name of it, I called it by description. Generational curses were not going to rule my life. My anger for my dad continued to grow. I felt like he dropped a bomb on me, at Christmas time, which has always been one of my favorite holidays, and then he left this world. He said that he wanted to make things right with me before he left. Making things right entails amending brokenness. There was no amending. Things were left broken. See... even with him, I had to face the truth. I had to deal with how he left me. I had to deal with the pain that was deep rooted. I remember screaming so loudly for God to free me of this. It was as if I was loosed in that moment. I felt a spiritual release. It wasn't over yet.

What was in it for me? The road to healing. The road to truly forgiving my dad. The road to releasing my fury. The road to freedom that I truly wanted

48

for me. I needed to move into a new space emotionally. My determination would not let me turn back. I was not going to keep going on this same path. The birth of the 80/20 Rule was established. I have lived by it ever since.

WHAT ELSE WAS IN IT FOR ME?

&EMINENT HEALING
&GROWTH
&FORGIVENESS: OF SELF, DAD, MOTHER, AND THESE MEN
&BOUNDARIES
&80/20 RULE
&DOING MY WORK
&ESTABLISHING GENERATIONAL BLESSINGS
&NOT A VICTIM TO MY CIRCUMSTANCES
&ALLOWING MYSELF TO BE FREE

From this moment forward, I was prepared to be single for the rest of my life if that is how I had to roll. I was set out to be better every day. I want for EVERY woman and man reading this book to understand what a child goes through, even into their adult life, when they don't take their parental stance in their child's life. The parental bond can be

broken when your presence isn't made known for your children. Trust might not ever be there, especially when lies, deceit, and lack of protection are factors of failure. Regardless of how they did me, I set out to be a much better parent and be present for my children. In conjunction, I set out to ride this ride solo. There was no more settling. No more compromising. I was done.

CHAPTER FIVE

The Emotional Pain

I went through enough emotional pain For a lifetime. I don't wish the turmoil that I've experienced on anyone. It's really difficult going through things when people see that you really have no one to turn to and no one shows up to fight on your behalf. I was in this fight by myself, even though my sister from another mother and another mister encouraged me and pushed me. She had her own things going on and I couldn't lean on her for everything. However, there was none of my biological family available to even help in anyway. The pain of feeling like a born failure seemed to haunt me most of my life. The pain of feeling like maybe God wouldn't ever bless me with a good man. In all honesty I did not know what a good man looked like. Those words from my dad's wife literally haunted me. My dad chose not to be there for me. I knew that I had to find a way. I knew that I had to get out of this particular cycle. I didn't know who I was. I did not know or understand my purpose. Even though I knew that settling for something less than what I want it was not exactly the best thing to do, it still haunted me.

Somewhere along the lines I knew that I had to make some more significant changes. I had to make changes that would be solid in that would not take me back into the same cycle of dating the same types of men. Even though

I feel like my father failed me, I still excepted responsibility for my choices in these men. As much as I wanted to blame my parents for their failures and their lack of caring for me, I still had to face the agonizing reality that I made a decision to deal with these men. Therefore, my forgiveness had to run even deeper for myself. I have to live with me. I don't have to live with any of them. Even though it wasn't easy to forgive my parents and the men who wronged me in these relationships, I still chose to. That in itself can be

painful in the process. If you understand what forgiveness is, then you understand why it is pertinent to move into a mindset of absolution. Dealing with the pain, forgiving them, and allowing them back into your personal space is three different things. Dealing with the pain has to do with acknowledging that it's there. The pain has caused you to feel ill emotions toward someone who has violated you in some form or fashion. It could be a breach of trust, it can be discord, or even a bad break up. Either way dealing with the pain of choices that you made or choices that were made against you is going to be difficult no matter how you look at it. It seems as though everywhere that I turned there was some type of upheaval. I was tired of being in pain. I can remember reading the prayer of Jabez. Jabez asked God to enlarge his territory. His promise to God was that he would not go about inflicting pain on anyone because he knew what pain felt like. He was born in pain.

1 Chronicles 4:9-10 (NKJV)
Now Jabez was more honorable than his brothers, and his mother
called his name Jabez, saying, "Because I bore him in pain."
And Jabez called on the God of Israel saying, "Oh, that
You would bless me indeed, and enlarge my territory,
that Your hand would be with me, and that You
would keep me from evil, that I may not cause pain!"
So God granted him what he requested.

I live by this even today. My thoughts on inflicting pain on someone else breaks my heart so I simply do not do it. My gran'mommy used to say, "It's not difficult to not hurt anyone. Just choose not to do it." Simple right? Not for many. Hurt people hurt people. I could have been one of those people because I sustained a lot of hurt in my life. I won't say that it was simple for me to choose not to hurt people. It was through prayer and fasting that I gained strength from God to let vengeance be His.

I had other things to do than to be revengeful towards people in my past. I had to do some soul searching. Things could not get any worse, at least that was my thought. I wanted my life to be better than what it had ever been. I went through some serious anger spells. Recalling the moment that my dad told me how he failed me sent me spiraling. I remember just crying out in screaming WHY... why would you have a

child in not be there for your child? I recalled moments when I pleaded with my daddy to be in a relationship with me. This pain, although it was every bit of emotional, had begun to attack my body. I felt worthless. I felt denied. I felt unloved. As I laid out on the floor recalling the agonizing moments of relationships that left me feeling empty, I cried out to God to heal me. Heal me from the wounds of every trauma that I've endured no matter where it came from. I asked God to let His strength be made perfect because I was weak. I am usually the one that everyone looks to as strong. Here I was percolating in weakness. What's worse is that I had no one to really turn to. I found myself alone after being there for so many other people. I had no one to be there for me. I was so emotionally fragile that I couldn't even be there for myself. My heart was broken. Psalm 51:17 (NIV) My sacrifice, O God, is a broken spirit; a broken and contrite heart you, God, will not despise. I know that God was near me. Even though the emotional distress was nearly unbearable, I found myself crying out even more to forgive my dad. I had to forgive him and release him. When I think back over those years and the moment that he decided to spill his truth I realized that even though I had forgiven him I never released him. It makes a difference.

One thing I can truly promise you is that it was not instantaneously. It was consistent prayer and staying focused on God's word and not allowing myself to sway back-and-forth into things that would take me out of here. It was so important for me to get it in this hour. I need it a change. I felt like Jacob and the angel when they were wrestling. I did not care what I had to do or how I had to do it I was not letting go of the hand of God anymore. He promised that he would never leave me nor forsake me and he held true to that. Every time something went on I was the one who took flight. But he saw fit to still love me and keep me even through this terrible amount of emotional pain that I went through. I was not letting go of Him and I wanted Him to change me and change me for good.

What I've learned in the midst of pain is not to focus on the pain but where the pain is pushing me to go and what it is pushing me to do. There was truly something different to come out of this. It is the same as the process of giving birth. You know the feeling when the baby's head is about to crown and you feel the most pressure that you have

ever felt in your pelvic floor. There is a heaviness that takes place as the baby is descending. As you push, the baby's head is coming through the ring of fire. Some of the pressure begins to release. Essentially, the baby is born. Your life will never be the same. I knew that I was not ever going to be the same. I was not going to look for a man, even though I never looked for Mr. Dressed Up In Lies, Mr. Totally Ambivalent, and Mr. Love Pistol. I wasn't going to make myself available for the drama anymore; not from them or anyone else. Even though I did not know what a good man looked like, I knew that God was going to bless me somehow. I also learned that we should be careful what we say God will and won't do especially using the word never.

I went through stages of pain and chose a distinguished path to heal.

1.   **Grief:** I grieved my issues as they were dying off. I allowed myself to feel the pain that haunted me. I had to in order to deal with the emotional trauma. I was once told by a doctor that you have to allow yourself the freedom to cry because it breaks barriers that will ultimately cause someone to be bitter and harbor unforgiveness. Therefore, I dug deep and grieved. I felt deserted and rejected. I was empty. I had given huge chunks of my heart to people who did not have good intentions and they never gave back. We were not in the same seasons of life to be able to have a solid rhythm and grow together. I didn't feel sorry for myself nor did I throw a pity party. Both of those non-friends would have sent me (you) spiraling. Thus, grieving is necessary in order to grow past your current situation. It is the exact same as grieving the death of someone you are close to. Grieve that thing and let go.

2.   **Anger:** I soon became angry. I was angry with myself for not having clear boundaries. I was angry with myself for not commanding the atmosphere and demanding my respect. I was angry with myself for not speaking up and defending myself; for allowing these men so many opportunities to get it right; for not saying what I felt right then and there, thus, letting it fester and eventually, going through this. I was even more angry because I didn't know how to do either. In my anger, I wanted to

retaliate so badly. However, I knew that it would only make matters worse. Consequently, IN MY ANGER, I asked God

to do His perfect will in their lives. I prayed this as often as it came to my mind. Not only did I cut Mr. Dressed Up In Lies, Mr. Totally Ambivalent, and Mr. Love Pistol off, I cut my dad's wife and stepdaughter and the rest of their children off. They served me no purpose. My anger soon faded out to something even bigger.

3.   **Acceptance:** I accepted my part in all of this with everyone. I was overwhelmed with trying to be accepted and gain their acceptance of me, that I was lost in the process. Thus, I accepted that this was just them and this is how they roll. They have made excuses for my feelings when I felt a certain way about their mother and the things that she did to me over my lifetime. "That's just momma," they say. So this is just me. So should the lack of respect for me be appropriate when their mother offends me because it's just her? No it should not. And so in the same manner, no excuses should be made for me or anyone else. So what because it is your mother or whoever. It has to be addressed regardless of who it is. So guess what? How they rolled didn't mesh with how I was rolling. Letting go was a must in order for me to move the way God needed me to. As I accepted my part in each situation, I wrote it out as part of the vision. This was placed under things that I did not want to see happen again. Some of the issues that I listed were people pleasing, falling for lies, not asking for discernment, allowing myself to be used, to be someone's dumping ground, and many more things. Acceptance is truly required, and definitely not easy. Grab some tissue because you might need it. But, you will be freed from the bondages that have been holding you hostage to the same behaviors for years with new faces attached to them.

4.   **Depression:** Ultimately, I suffered from depression. This may or may not be everyone's reality. However, it was my reality. I owned it and sought help for it. If you know that you are experiencing symptoms of depression, please do not wallow in it. Own it and seek help. Some of the symptoms include, but not limited to:

Mood: anxiety, apathy, general discontent, guilt, hopelessness, loss of interest or pleasure in activities, mood swings, or sadness
Behavioral: agitation, excessive crying, irritability, restlessness, or social isolation

Sleep: early awakening, excess sleepiness, insomnia, or restless sleep
Whole body: excessive hunger, fatigue, or loss of appetite
Cognitive: lack of concentration, slowness in activity, or thoughts of suicide
Weight: weight gain or weight loss
Also common: poor appetite or repeatedly going over thoughts
(Mayo Clinic, 2020).
Do not be afraid to seek help. It doesn't mean that you are crazy. It means that you are attending to your mental health just as you would attend to your physical health. Both are vitally important and you need them to function as normal as possible. Depression symptoms may not solely show up because of a bad relationship, a breakup, or toxic relationships. However, these relationships may be contributing factors along with other events that have taken place in your life and sometimes, it may stem from childhood. Regardless of how you became depressed, seek treatment. Think of it this way, a person can scrape his/her knee running or roller skating. Regardless of how the scrape got there, it still needs to be cleaned and treated. Don't deprive yourself of the healing process.

5.   **Desolation:** This is truly difficult. You start to feel as though no one cares about how you feel. They don't understand. They have a remedy for you, but since you don't want to do things their way, they don't want to deal with you. In some cases, people will point the finger at you in a "Ah ha" manner or a "that's what you get" manner. Desolation can lead to isolation. You feel ashamed. You don't want to be around people because they don't support you in love and in truth. This is an extremely empty and lonely time. However, it is what I experienced. It was easier to stay home and chill out in my room. I hung out with my circle every now and again, but that was it.

6.   **Disconnectedness:** I had no one. My circle knew what was going on, but they couldn't help me. They were there as much as they could be. However, they had their own lives. They had their own set of personal issues that they had to deal with. Socially, I had no one to connect with who could mentor me or help me out of this rut.

What Did I Feel?
I went through each one of these phases dreadfully. As painful as it was, I had to acknowledge each level of pain. I had to be honest with myself. It was a feeling like being in labor with no drugs. It hurt badly.

I chose not to turn to the bottle or to dope. I have heard that people often drink and smoke drugs because they have problems. But the problems still exists when you sober up. So, I had to put my shero cape on and get ready to tackle each problem head on. I didn't care how much crying that I had to do I was going to get through it. I prayed every time the issues came to my mind. I felt anxious at times. Sometimes I was nauseated. I already suffer from migraines. Some days were more difficult than others.

I knew that I was in the fight of my life. I was fighting to remove generational curses. I was fighting to remove the curses of my forefathers. I was fighting to break soul-ties. I wanted to create generational blessings. I wanted to create generational wealth. I wanted a legacy. I wasn't quite sure how I was going to get there. The one person who I thought was my bestie for life even did me in. I was out done. CHANGE WAS EMINENT I tell ya. There was no way that I wanted to live in this space. Part of the desolation and disconnectedness was to avoid being kicked while I was already down. Remember you cannot kick someone who is already down. They are already at the bottom of their barrel and don't need your foot to help them get down any further.

I even found myself wondering what if this was some weird twilight zone and felt stuck. Either way, I was pushing past my thoughts and emotions. I remember going to church one Mother's Day. There was an African pastor who was preaching. He preached on the widow who had the son and the prophet Elisha gave her a set of instructions, 2 Kings 4. As he preached, I felt the anointing fall on me. I was so full of the Holy Spirit on that day. I felt like I had enough strength to run through that place like Flo Jo. I was still in emotional pain, but I was closer to my healing. I was walking in a different manner. I was determined to come out of the lion's den smelling like a rose. I was determined to get beauty for my ashes. I was not going to lay down and die. Just like the widow, I had work to do. She could have laid down and died, but she followed the wisdom of the prophet and God blessed her tremendously. I asked for wisdom. I asked for direction. I made plans and sought first the kingdom of heaven. It took me long enough to get to this point. I was at a point of no return. Remember, I felt like Jacob when he wrestled with the angel. I was not going to let
up until God changed me. I started seeing it. The pain was finally diminishing. Even though I was still going through the fire, I never gave up on getting out of pain.

There is no mistaking that pain is just that: PAIN. My goal was to get out of it and get out of it permanently. I worked hard to maintain a Positive Attitude In Negativity. When everything fails, change your perspective on how you are viewing your situation. I couldn't remove the pain the way I wanted to. I changed how I viewed it. I chose to remain positive. I chose not to focus on where I was in my situation. I chose to see the end. I asked God to show me ME the way He sees me. I needed to see it through His eyes. I was able to see myself as a finished product. As I viewed myself as a finished product, I began to move in such a way that my healing was fluid.

Settling and Compromising: Enough is ENOUGH

I remember making a call to my cousin in Georgia. I was in tears. I was in emotional pain. She cried with me. Then she prayed. She prayed over me and she prayed for me. She asked God to please bless me with the kind of love that He blessed her within her husband. In the midst of praying, she said, "The Holy Spirit just gave me something for you." I love when the Holy Spirit has something for me. She said, "He said to let you know don't settle and don't compromise. DON'T SETTLE AND DON'T COMPROMISE." Tears started pouring from my eyes. It was a sigh of relief. It was what I needed to hear. I owned the moment. I knew that God's mercy reigned and rained down on me.

When I began my journey to healing, in the midst of it all, I reflected on where I settled and where I compromised. First thing that I know I settled and compromised is this dude's height. I am short, but he was shorter than me. I like tall men. He is an attractive man, but that doesn't do anything for me when he is character flawed. He wasn't as giving as I am. He wasn't open hearted. He was a user. He was unfaithful and not loyal. He lied and tried to manipulate me. I reported to my counselor this information from my cousin. She agreed wholeheartedly. She explained to me that every time I settle and compromise, I lose more and more of myself and it becomes that much
more difficult to find myself. I didn't care how bad things may have gotten, I was determined not to settle and not to compromise. I established a plan for myself and did not deviate from it. I tried to date one guy after this. He didn't know how to order from a menu at a restaurant and thought that I was going to be his shugga momma. He was in for a rude awakening and got the business really quick. He was dismissed with no further action. He

called me repeatedly until I had the phone company block his number. I was so empowered, even though I was still dealing with my pain. I wasn't afraid to lose or walk away.

James 1:22-25 (ESV)
But be doers of the word, and not hearers only, deceiving yourselves. For if anyone is a hearer of the word and not a doer, he is like a man who looks intently at his natural face in a mirror. For he looks at himself and goes away and at once forgets what he was like. But the one who looks into the perfect law, the law of liberty, and perseveres, being no hearer who forgets but a doer who acts, he will be blessed in his doing.

I had to choose to look into the perfect law of liberty after this situationship blew up in my face. Looking back, I'm not mad at him for being himself. I was angry with myself for not following the lead of the Holy Spirit. I was angry with myself for not moving out of the situation when I was presented with the unction in my spirit. Overall, even though I allowed myself to stay in this situationship, I thank God for being a forgiving God, for being merciful and for giving me his grace. I am harder on myself in most cases. In this case, it was difficult but I was fed up and I womaned up.

Tenets of Truth

1. **Do not allow yourself to be blinded by what you want vs. reality.** *Proverbs 12:19 (KJV) The lip of truth shall be established for ever: but a lying tongue is but for a moment.*

2. **Do not be afraid to walk away when you are in a different**

   season than someone else. If it isn't working, you alone can't make it work. *2 Corinthians 6:14 (AMPC) Do not be unequally yoked with unbelievers and do not make mismated alliances with them or come under a different yoke with them, inconsistent with your faith. For what partnership have right living and right standing with God with iniquity and lawlessness? Or how can light have fellowship with darkness?*

3. **The signs you see are there to protect you.** When you see the signs, don't deny the truth that is within. Eventually, this will blow

up in your face. **Proverbs 16:18 (CEB)** *Pride comes before disaster, and arrogance before a fall.*

4. **DO NOT settle and DO NOT compromise.** *Hebrews 10:26 (ESV) For if we go on sinning deliberately after receiving the knowledge of the truth, there no longer remains a sacrifice for sins.*

5. **Explore self-care.** You are the only you that you have. You have to take care of you. If you can't, don't or won't take care of you, who will? You are responsible for you. *Mark 6:31-32 (TLB) Then Jesus suggested, "Let's get away from the crowds for a while and rest." For so many people were coming and going that they scarcely had time to eat. So they left by boat for a quieter spot.*

Take these tenets of truth and apply them to your life. Do not continue to live in the deceit of lies just because you witnessed your family and friends go through things that might not have been successful. Do not do things a certain way just because you witnessed "momma doing it." By this, I am truly referring to things that are unhealthy, things that have caused hurt, harm and danger, and things that you know are not right yet you continue in the process until you are deeply and emotionally hurt. You do not have to live in the past. You are not subjected and enslaved to your past unless you choose to be. However, you will have to deal with the past in order to move on from
it. Do not get caught up in generational indispositions. You have the right, by your Father who is in heaven, to be a generational blessing maker and a generational wealth creator. Create a newness. The bible tells us in Romans 12:2 (NIV) Do not conform to the pattern of this world, but be transformed by the renewing of your mind. Then you will be able to test and approve what God's will is—his good, pleasing, and perfect will. What more do you know is required of you? Nothing changes unless you change them.

Self-care

The true satisfaction starts and completes with God and having Him first. Now, I was single and was learning me, it was time for self-care. Self-care is often understood as going to a salon to get hair and nails done or getting a massage. While these are wonderful aspects of self-care, it goes much deeper. Self-care has to do with redefining who you are, especially after breaking up with someone, even if the someone was a friend. You have to protect your happiness, improve your physical and mental health and your well-being. Self-care encompasses some of the following:

1.　　**Spirituality** – Joshua 1:8 (AMP) This Book of the Law shall not depart from my mouth, but I shall read and meditate on it day and night, so that I may be careful to do everything in accordance with all that is written in it; for then I will make my way prosperous, and then I will be a good success.

2.　　**Physical Self-care** – 1 Corinthians 3:16-17 (CSB) Don't you yourselves know that you are God's temple and that the Spirit of God lives in you? If anyone destroys God's temple, God will destroy him; for God's temple is holy, and that is what you are.

3.　　**Psychological Self-care** – Proverbs 11:14 (NKJV) Where there is no counsel, the people fall; But in the multitude of counselors there is safety.

4.　　**Emotional Self-care** – Philippians 4:8 (KJV) Finally, brethren, whatsoever things are true, whatsoever things are honest, whatsoever things are just, whatsoever things are pure, whatsoever things are lovely, whatsoever things are of good report; if there be any virtue, and if there be any praise, think on these things.

5.　　**Occupational** – Colossians 3:23 (ESV) Whatever you do, work heartily, as for the Lord and not for men...

6.　　**Social** – John 13:34-35 (ESV) A new commandment I give to you, that you love one another: just as I have loved you, you also are to love one another. By this all people will know that you are my disciples if you have love for one another."

7.　　**Intellectual** - Luke 12:48 (NKJV) But he who did not know, yet committed things deserving of stripes, shall be beaten with few. For everyone to whom much is given, from him much will be required; and to whom much has been committed, of him they will ask the more.

This is a Self-care Wheel. I created it with biblical scriptures that coordinate with the one created by Olga Phoenix. This is a guide to understanding how you can add true self-care into your life. The bonus is that going to salons are the extra needed treats.

Remember, you are the only you that you have. You have to take care of you. If you can't, don't or won't take care of you, who will? You are responsible for you. You are worthy of your own love. If you don't feel worthy of your own love, why should anyone else? Thus, I embraced learning who I am. I welcomed the action to forgive myself and forgive Mr. Love Pistol and the other two. I had to release the anger that I held against my dad. For the longest, he lived a lie where I was concerned. Some part of me wished that he had taken the lies to his grave because regardless of his failures, I thought he was my hero. When he made his confession to me before his demise, it broke me even more.

Nonetheless, I owned my part in the situation. It was hard, but I embraced it. I refused to play the victim. In order for me to be healed, I had to be honest with myself and see the truth for what it was. The goal is to see the truth for what it is rather than for what it was. I wanted to be emotionally healthy. Therefore, I dealt with my issues. In my pursuit to eminent change and healing, I reassessed the situation one last time before reestablishing my boundaries. I wrote the pros and cons of the relationship. I made my way to setting my 80/20 Rule. I learned that I actually like me. I learned to love me. I fell in love with me. There was no stopping me and I was on this journey. It got so good that a friend and I started hanging out and treated ourselves to some of the classiest restaurants from Beverly Hills to Costa Mesa. We enjoyed doing something for us. We were determined to have good and better quality relationships that had meaning and purpose. It all started with saying "YES" to His will. I know that I was doing my homework and was destined to be the best me that I could be and exceptionally for me. The man who I would marry would get all of the benefits of the healed me, the changed me. Ultimately, my change was for God. He needed to use me and all for His glory.

CHAPTER SIX

The Excellent Plan

The excellent plan could not present itself until God had my full attention. I was done with dancing with darkness. I was done entering into relationships that served only one person. I was done with relationships that were/are not mutually beneficial. His excellent plan for me would only present itself when I was attentive to that which the Holy Spirit wanted to teach me. His excellent plan couldn't take precedence in my life until I surrendered me to Him. I surrendered my will to His will. I wasn't sure what this was going to look like in its totality in the end, but I promised to trust Him throughout this transition. Jeremiah 29:11 (AMPC) says for I know the thoughts and plans that I have for you, says the Lord, thoughts and plans for welfare and peace and not for evil, to give you hope in your final outcome.

Even though I didn't have all of the details, I was determined to move according to His plan and His will. I soon realized that there was going to be a vibrant testimony to come forth. In this stage, I was still doing my work to heal. There were so many years of hell that I had to heal from. There was no way that I was going to get through it in a few short months.

Here are some choices that I made to move into the greatness that He had for me.

1.   **Cut communication:** relationships that are not mutually beneficial will serve no purpose for you. This was an essential part of the process. It was needed in order to move into my healing place.

2.   **Choose honesty:** no matter how bad your situation gets, be honest with yourself. Do not water down the truth about needing help to change your path. Be honest with those who hurt you. If they refuse to accept responsibility for their actions, that is none of your business. If you know that speaking to those who hurt you will not bring about a resolution, forgive anyway and leave them in the hands of God and worry no more.

3.   **FORGIVENESS:** go into this phase openhearted and willing. You are not giving your offender a pass or saying that what they did is alright. You are releasing them from a place that they cannot be held in. For example, if you harbor unforgiveness, you hold yourself hostage. The offenders are still out there offending. Another reason to forgive is to understand that they didn't possess the capacity to love and care for you the way you needed them to. That includes my parents. Forgiveness does not mean that there is an open door policy and the offender(s) can return at any time. Forgiveness is releasing them from a space that is meant to love, have compassion, and freedom. It is also understanding that they are broken people and they couldn't give anything more than what they had, even when they choose not to do the right thing.

4.   **Love thyself:** loving yourself is complicated when you never learned how to do it. Loving yourself entails the following:

a.   ***Understand what love is*** - 1 Corinthians 13:4-8 (AMP)
Love endures with patience and serenity, love is kind and thoughtful, and is not jealous or envious; love does not brag and is not proud or arrogant. It is not rude; it is not self-seeking; it is not provoked nor overly sensitive and easily angered; it does not take into account a wrong endured. It does not rejoice at injustice but rejoices with the truth when right and truth prevail. Love bears all things regardless of what comes, believes all things

looking for the best in each one, hopes all things remaining steadfast during difficult times, endures all things without weakening. Love never fails it never fades nor ends. But as for prophecies, they will pass away; as for tongues, they will cease; as for the gift of special knowledge, it will pass away.

b.   ***Establishing boundaries*** - Setting clear personal boundaries is the key to ensuring relationships are mutually respectful, supportive, and caring. Boundaries are a measure of self-esteem. Weak boundaries leave you vulnerable and likely to be taken for granted or even damaged by others. On the other hand, a healthy self-respect will produce boundaries which show you deserve to be treated well. They also will protect you from exploitative relationships and help you avoid getting too close to people who don't have your best interests at heart (Collingwood, 2018).

c.   ***Learn who you are*** - Jeremiah 1:5 (AMPC)
Before I formed you in the womb I knew and approved of you as My chosen instrument, and before you were born I separated and set you apart, consecrating you; and I appointed you as a prophet to the nations.

5.   **Learning what you like** – You can conduct a Personal SWOT Analysis on yourself. A personal SWOT Analysis is a powerful tool that you can use to hone in on your strengths, weaknesses, opportunities, and strengths within yourself. See the end of the book on how you can grab a free copy of the Personal SWOT Analysis sheets for free. Write your likes and dislikes about yourself. Include things like your favorite color(s), foods, restaurants, shopping, travel, etc. after you write these down, include the "WHY" for each one. Your list isn't exhaustive and may change over time. This is getting to know you and what you like and what you do not like.

6.   **Develop mutually beneficial relationships** – reflect on the section about boundaries. DO NOT allow yourself to enter into any more relationships that do not serve both parties mutually. DO NOT allow yourself to be taken by anyone no matter how good it looks, talk, walk, or smell. Pray and ask for discernment if you are struggling in this area. 1 John 4:1; Philippians 1:9-10; Hebrews 4:12

6.   **Treat yourself** – take yourself to have a spa day or do something fun and spontaneous, and of course, something safe. Go out to eat at an upscale restaurant. Be observant. Make sure you smile and look happy. Faith it until you make it. It's not about being alone as much as it is self-discovery. You will learn to not only love and appreciate yourself, but you are setting the tone for how you will allow and want someone else to treat you.

8.   **Teach others how to treat you** - When someone does something to offend you, address it as soon as possible, preferably right then and there. This has been one of the biggest struggles for me. I have often kept a closed mouth when it comes to addressing the issues right then and there. I promised myself that I would no longer keep a closed mouth when it comes to my feelings and how someone addresses me insensitively. If they feel the need to open their mouth and say what they feel, I have the right address it and correct it. I mean... it doesn't have to be done in a Sheneneh Jenkins kinda way. It can be done in a sassy, professional way with a little Sheneneh twist on it. LOL!

What Did I Learn?

With His excellent plan for my life, I learned to love me. I learned to reevaluate and reassess my boundaries. In reevaluating and reassessing, I reestablished my boundaries. I chose not to bend on them. I learned to take care of myself. I mastered this so well that when I did meet the Mr. Right for Me, he would automatically know how to treat me without me saying a word. I learned the essentials of setting the tone for my life. I positioned myself to stay in a position of learning so that I can progress continuously throughout my life. The emotional pain that I endured positioned me to work towards courageousness, empowerment, and fearlessness.

Courageousness: I was able to exhibit bravery to conquer my issues head on. From brokenness to forgiveness, forgiveness of self, to loving myself and keeping my boundaries tight. Deuteronomy 31:6 (AMPC) says be strong, courageous, and firm; fear not nor be in terror before them, for it is the Lord your God Who goes with you; He will not fail you or forsake you. Things could have been a lot worse.

Empowerment: 2 Corinthians 12:9 (AMPC) says He said to me, My grace, My favor, loving-kindness, and mercy, is enough for you.

sufficient against any danger and enables you to bear the trouble manfully; for My strength and power are made perfect, fulfilled, and completed, and show themselves most effective in your weakness. Therefore, I will all the more gladly glory in my weaknesses and infirmities, that the strength and power of Christ, the Messiah, may rest (yes, may pitch a tent over and dwell) upon me! I had to find strength that only comes from the Lord to make it through. There was no other way to do it. If you recall, in my moment of emotional pain, I had no one. I pressed in harder and harder to the strength of God. I knew that His strength was made perfect just for me.

Fearlessness: I remember having to get up and take control of my life and move in boldness by myself. This was never a huge problem for me until going through this tough situation. My confidence level increased as I overcame obstacle after obstacle. I gave God the glory every step of the way. When I think of fearlessness, two scriptures come to mind. 2 Timothy 1:7 (CEV) God's Spirit doesn't make cowards out of us. The Spirit gives us power, love, and self-control. Isaiah 41:10 (ESV) fear not, for I am with you; be not dismayed, for I am your God; I will strengthen you, I will help you, I will uphold you with my righteous right hand.

Ultimately, I realized that this too shall pass. I was not destined to live in failure. I was destined for greatness. I have been telling my children and grandchildren for the past four years that they are destined for greatness. This is because He said that He did not make us cowards. We were not born with the spirit of fear. I had a job to do that would further enhance His kingdom and it did not entail bringing along slackers. When I look back at what I went through during this time, I realize that He had a calling on my life. He chose me. He knew that I would go forward and tell it. I learned that in being courageous, empowering myself through His word, and being fearless that I am call to teach and speak to the hearts of the masses who struggle with building solid relationships. My suffering was not in vain.

CHAPTER SEVEN

The Comprehensive Process

Ahhhhh! So here we are. I am so excited about this section. My level of excitement is because many of us do not understand the process. Many of us do not want to go through the process. In all honesty, the process hurts the most. Reflect for a moment on the process that a baby goes through to be born. If you have not had the birthing experience, pay close attention.

According to the Mayo Clinic, there are three stages to the birthing process.

Stage 1 – In the first stage of labor and birth occurs when you begin to feel regular contractions, which cause the cervix to open (dilate) and soften, shorten, and thin (effacement). This allows the baby to move into the birth canal. The first stage is the longest of the three stages. It's actually divided into two phases of its own — early labor (latent phase) and active labor.

Early labor

During early labor, your cervix dilates and effaces. You'll feel mild, irregular contractions. As your cervix begins to open, you might notice a clear, pink, or slightly bloody discharge from your vagina. This is likely the mucus plug that blocks the cervical opening during pregnancy.

How long it lasts: Early labor is unpredictable. For first-time moms, the average length varies from hours to days. It's often shorter for subsequent deliveries.

What you can do: Until your contractions increase in frequency and intensity, it's up to you. For many women, early labor isn't particularly uncomfortable. Try to stay relaxed.

To promote comfort during early labor:

- Go for a walk
- Take a shower or bath
- Listen to relaxing music
- Try breathing or relaxation techniques taught in childbirth class
- Change positions

Your health care provider will instruct you on when to leave for the hospital or birthing center. If your water breaks or you experience significant vaginal bleeding, call your health care provider right away.

Active labor

Now it's time for the real work to begin. During active labor, your cervix will dilate from 6 centimeters (cm) to 10 cm. Your contractions will become stronger, closer together and regular. Your legs might cramp, and you might feel nauseated. You might feel your water break — if it hasn't already — and experience increasing pressure in your back. If you haven't headed to your labor and delivery facility yet, now's the time.

Don't be surprised if your initial excitement wanes as labor progresses and the pain intensifies. Ask for pain medication or anesthesia if you want it. Your health care team will partner with you to make the best choice for you and your baby. Remember, you're the only one who can judge your need for pain relief.

How long it lasts: Active labor often lasts four to eight hours or more. On average, your cervix will dilate at approximately one centimeter per hour.

What you can do: Look to your labor coach and health care team for encouragement and support. Try breathing and relaxation techniques to combat your growing discomfort. Use what you learned in childbirth class or ask your health care team for suggestions.

Unless you need to be in a specific position to allow for close monitoring of you and your baby, consider these ways to promote comfort during active labor:

Change positions

- Roll on a large rubber ball (birthing ball)
- Take a warm shower or bath
- Take a walk, stopping to breathe through contractions
- Have a gentle massage between contractions
- If you need to have a C-section, having food in your stomach can lead to complications. If your health care provider thinks you might need a C-section, he or she might recommend small amounts of clear liquids, such as water, ice chips, popsicles, and juice, instead of a large, solid meal.

The last part of active labor – often referred to as transition – can be particularly intense and painful. Contractions will come close together and can last 60 to 90 seconds. You'll experience pressure in your lower back and rectum. Tell your health care provider if you feel the urge to push.

If you want to push but you're not fully dilated, your health care provider might ask you to hold back. Pushing too soon could make you tired and cause your cervix to swell, which might delay delivery. Pant or blow your way through the contractions. Transition usually lasts 15 to 60 minutes.

Stage 2: The birth of your baby

It's time! You'll deliver your baby during the second stage of labor.

How long it lasts: It can take from a few minutes up to a few hours or more to push your baby into the world. It might take longer for first-time moms and women who've had an epidural.

What you can do: Push! Your health care provider will ask you to bear down during each contraction or tell you when to push. Or you might be asked to push when you feel the need.

When you push, don't hold tension in your face. Bear down and concentrate on pushing where it counts. If possible, experiment with different positions until you find one that feels best. You can push while squatting, sitting, kneeling – even on your hands and knees.

At some point, you might be asked to push more gently – or not at all. Slowing down gives your vaginal tissues time to stretch rather than tear. To stay motivated, you might ask to feel the baby's head between your legs or see it in a mirror.

After your baby's head is delivered, the rest of the baby's body will follow shortly. His or her airway will be cleared if necessary. Your health care provider or labor coach will then cut the umbilical cord.

Stage 3: Delivery of the placenta

After your baby is born, you'll likely feel a great sense of relief. You might hold the baby in your arms or on your abdomen. Cherish the moment. But a lot is still happening. During the third stage of labor, you will deliver the placenta.

How long it lasts: The placenta is typically delivered in five to 30 minutes, but the process can last as long as an hour.

What you can do: Relax! By now your focus has likely shifted to your baby. You might be oblivious to what's going on around you. If you'd like, try breast-feeding your baby.

You'll continue to have mild contractions. They'll be close together and less painful. You'll be asked to push one more time to deliver the placenta. You might be given medication before or after the placenta is delivered to encourage uterine contractions and minimize bleeding.

Your health care provider will examine the placenta to make sure it's intact. Any remaining fragments must be removed from the uterus to prevent bleeding and infection. If you're interested, ask to see the placenta.

After you deliver the placenta, this is essentially a second delivery, your uterus will continue to contract to help it return to its normal size. A member of your health care team will massage your abdomen to make sure the uterus feels firm. Your health care provider will also determine whether you need stitches or repair of any tears of your vaginal region. If you don't have anesthesia, you'll receive an injection of local anesthetic in the area to be stitched (Cunningham, et al., 2020).

The process. This is only one part of the entire birthing process. From the moment of conception, the three stages of the trimesters and the finale, and the birthing process, all comprise the makeup of the baby. This is the natural process. There are some who have to deliver via C-Section. There are also those who have challenges conceiving for one reason or another. Their processes are very different. However, they achieve the same results in the end: the baby.

The physical pain associated with each one is a process and story in itself. If you interview 1,000 women who were in the process of giving birth, they will either tell you that they are having no pain or their pain is so monstrous that it is something that is indescribable. Although the processes can vary for giving birth, regardless of the method of delivery, every woman's experience is different, even if she has multiple children. This is a process that is TOTALLY unavoidable. It has to happen. there is no going around it. When a baby is stillborn, the mother still has to give birth. IT HAS TO HAPPEN. This is the same thing that we go through when we want something different from God.

Whether you were born in failure, born in pain, or born with a silver spoon in your mouth, you have the ability to pick up a pen and rewrite your destiny. Whatever the process is that got you here is not as important as the fact that you are here. You are breathing. You have the right to change your destiny. DO NOT try to avoid the process. It is necessary. It is there for your growth. It is there for God to get the glory from your pain. You might ask, "Wha'chu talkin'about Keci? (in your Gary Coleman voice)." See, you just might have been born to fail. You just might have been born to lose, at least in the eyes of the world. The first thing that you have to understand is that your parents may not have had what you needed to help you do what was needed for you to do more than survive in this world. They may have been broken people who sought wholeness from one another. They just didn't have it. The second thing is to realize that the devil always wants us to believe lies. However, Genesis 50:20 (ESV) tells us as for you, you meant evil against me, but God meant it for good, to bring it about that many people should be kept alive, as they are today. YOU WILL SEE A VICTORY! Rewrite your destiny sis. It is not too late. Thirdly, deal with your past. Don't run from it. If there are people in your past who are too toxic to resolve issues with, pray for them and move on. if you feel that you need to speak with them, ask God for such an appointed time. Otherwise, move on and call it a day.

"The Process is NEVER Pretty,"

Therefore,

Appreciate the Process

it is NEVER pretty
but it is imperative that we go through it
to get to the

Crown of Beauty

that will be exchanged for ashes...
Isaiah 61:3
by

Keci Monique'

Appreciating the process is mandatory. Appreciating it means that you have come to the fruition that you are in the midst of changing. You are in the mandate of growth. Your destiny is changing direction. You realize that you do not have to be what everyone said you were (in the negative sense). Appreciate your process.

The process is never pretty. Think about the birthing process. Back in the day, television had all of us fooled into thinking that babies were delivered all pretty and cleaned up and dropped off by the stork. No such a thang (in my Harpo voice from The Color Purple). The birthing process is extremely messy. There are bodily fluids that are expelled. The scent is quite disgusting. The baby is covered in a white layer called vernix caseosa, which

protects their skin from the constant exposure to amniotic fluid in the womb. It is there until it is washed off with their first bath. Once the baby is cleaned up and dressed, the process has been completed. There is still healing to do, but the process... appreciate it. It cannot be avoided. It is imperative that we go through it. It will be painful at times. That pain can be emotional, physical or both. BUT there is a Crown of Beauty that you will receive for your pain. This is your garment of praise.

You can do this sis! Don't quit. Your testimony is depending on it. You have an audience waiting to hear your story. Don't quit in the midst of your process. God is right there as He promised.

If you are a man and you are reading this, even though you can't physically go through the birthing process, the principle is the same. You get pregnant with desire. You get pregnant with vision. Don't abandon the process. You will be stuck for a lifetime or at least until you go through the process.

CHAPTER EIGHT

The Divine Purpose

Why did I go through everything that I went through? A good deal of it was my parents fault. A good deal of it was the devil's fault. The rest was my fault. Because God destined me for greatness, I was able to see that I needed to rewrite my destiny. He knew that I wanted to be married. He knew that I would honor Him with my marriage. He knew that we would honor Him together. The divine purpose is for me to tell you that it is not too late for love if you want it. Healthy relationships can be yours. Being in love with someone who is genuinely in love with you can be yours. You might say, "I was hurt by my significant other in previous relationships." So was I. "My parents were this or that." So were mine. "My hurt is too deep." So was mine. You have to deal with it. Dig that stuff out and move forward. Go back to the chapter where I talked about the stages of pain that I went through and chose a distinguished path to heal. The divine purpose is for God's name to be declared in ALL of the earth. Romans 9:17 (ESV) tell us For the Scripture says to Pharaoh, "For this very purpose I have raised you up, that I might show my power in you, and that my name might be proclaimed in all the earth." Will you move into God's divine purpose for your life today?

Empowerment Moment:

Everything that you have gone through in this life was not in vain. You have gone through it to tell someone else. You will help others with your story. I get it... some stories are worse than others. Some may be difficult to understand. Regardless, there is someone in this world who needs you to show up and show out with your testimony. Can you remember sitting in class and feeling ashamed to ask a question for fear that it might be stupid? It is the same concept. The only stupid question is the one that isn't asked. The only way that you will help someone is to tell your story. It's not for the purposes of telling your business. You don't have to give every single detail. However, you do have to be transparent. Pray and ask God to lead and guide you.

Fulfilling God's divine purpose is work. You are showing those who need your testimony that there is an opportunity to be courageous, to be empowered, and to be fearless. You are an overcomer. *"When peace, like a river, attendeth my way, When sorrows like sea billows roll; Whatever my lot, Thou has taught me to say, It is well, it is well, with my soul,"* (Horatio Gates Spafford, 1873). God never promised us that it will be easy. James 1:2 (NLT) Faith and Endurance: Dear brothers and sisters, when troubles of any kind come your way, consider it an opportunity for great joy. We can't always see the end of what we are going through because of where we are in the process. This was the case with me. I couldn't see the beauty that was going to arise out of my situation. I only looked at my here and now. There is something greater to come from every challenge.

How can you determine that there is something greater to come from all of your challenges? Here are some questions to consider:

1. What is the lesson in my trial and tribulation?
2. Who will this benefit in the end besides me?
3. How can my voice be heard as a result of what I am going through?
4. My biggest challenge in life has been _____ ?
5. How intense is my pain?

77

6. What is God's plan?
7. I will go through the process with the strength of God.
8. What is the purpose?

As you answer these questions for yourself, focus on this :

a.   A Lesson Learned is a Lesson That Won't Return (Pastor W. Garrett)
      No matter what, go forth and purpose to learn a lesson from everything that you go through. You might not always get it right on the first round. When you see that something is posing as a challenge, brace yourself, take notes and ask yourself those eight questions listed above. Ask the Holy Spirit to teach you how to recognize and discern these things when they come upon and how to deal with them as they come. Do this so that you don't spend years in a cycle that is difficult to break when so much time has passed.

b.   Wisdom, Knowledge and Understanding
      In all thy getting, get understanding. Proverbs 4:7 (NKJV) 7 Wisdom is the principal thing.
      Therefore get wisdom. And in all your getting, get understanding. No matter what goes on, do not live life without getting an understanding of your who, what, when, where, how and why of every situation. You may not understand initially. 2 Peter 3:18 (NKJV) says but grow in the grace and knowledge of our Lord and Savior Jesus Christ. To Him be the glory both now and forever. Amen.

His divine purpose will be fulfilled one way or another. Remember Jonah? He ran from his calling. Jonah 1:1-3 (NKJV) Jonah's Disobedience: Now the word of the Lord came to Jonah the son of Amittai, saying, "Arise, go to Nineveh, that great city, and cry out

78

against it; for their wickedness has come up before Me." But Jonah arose to flee to Tarshish from the presence of

the Lord. He went down to Joppa, and found a ship going to

Tarshish; so he paid the fare, and went down into it, to go with them to Tarshish from the presence of the Lord. Do you know when the Lord is giving you instructions? Okay, I didn't know at first either. I had to learn to hear His still small voice. When you are unsure of an assignment from the Lord, ask Him for confirmation. He knows very well how to confirm to you what He means all by Himself.

So, you know that Jonah ended up in the belly of the huge fish. Are you in the belly of the huge fish right now? This is a miserable place to be. Don't be like Jonah. Cry out to God to teach you what His divine plan for your life is if you do not know. He will show you. He will make your name great. He will do for you what you have done for others. His divine purpose is going to be completed in all of the earth.

CHAPTER NINE

My Boaz

Where It All Started

After dealing with everything that I had gone through: the pain, understanding the plan, realizing the process, and heeding to the divine purpose of God, I took time to get to know me and do things for me that I specifically liked for me. I started hanging out with a coworker and we started having our friend days where she and I would treat ourselves to fancy restaurants, nail salons and made plans to do more stuff. I came to the realization that I really missed Georgia.

I decided to start planning my relocation back. Originally, I left Compton, California in July 2002. I felt like God wanted me to move away from my family as He did with Abraham. I felt as though He was telling me to move away from everything that was familiar and move to a place that He will show me. I moved on my faith and started my expedition to a better quality of life. I lived in Southeast Georgia for approximately five years. I had to go back to help my gran'mommy. She was in the beginning stages of dementia. I moved back to California in 2007. Gran'mommy lived in Compton all of my life. I was very familiar and I fit right in. I found a job within two weeks of being home. I was on my usual rise and grind. This was the time that I was spending completing my undergraduate degree. I transferred to DeVry University. I was working on my degree in Criminal Justice. This was satisfying to me. I saw myself in a longstanding career and was looking forward to all of it. I soon obtained a position with Los Angeles County Probation Department as a Juvenile Corrections Officer. About nine months in I was injured on the job. I had no idea what my future would entail and how everything would unfold.

After all of the rubbish of my last situationship that I thought was a relationship, I was no longer bound to the idea of just having a relationship. I set those boundaries and my 80/20 Rule and DID NOT BEND on them. There were a lot of men coming for me. None met my standards... that is until September 26th, 2010. My cousin made a post on social media. She was going through some things and was at her breaking point according to the post.

The post went like this:
Jenee` Harris: "is BENDING and trying not to BREAK! Lord it's NOT easy.... I think I'm at my breaking point.
Jerome Reynolds responds at 10:00 p.m., "I hope not."
Gaw'ga Peechy Keen responds saying, "Be like a tree planted by rivers of running waters. It bends, but it never breaks... it only grows. You can do it and get through it because God's strength is made perfect in our weakness.
That post came through at 10:03 p.m. By 10:06 p.m.
Jerome Reynolds says, "Well-spoken @mskeen u have some pretty feet.
Gaw'ga Peechy Keen replied, "Thank you very much. I keep them together."
Jerome Reynolds: An it shows.
Cousin finally chimes in, "lol... now that put a much needed smile on my face. Jerome u crazy..lol..and I thank all of u 4 ur encouraging words...

I received a friend request from Jerome Reynolds during the first week of October 2010. I had just gotten my nails done that day. Typically what I would do is post a picture of my nails or my feet. He was completely astonished. Six months prior to this I was in a situationship with a man who was not what I needed. I was out of place and I knew it. Six months prior to this conversation with Jerome, I thought I had

met someone I could deal with long-term. However, dealing with someone was a form of settling and compromising. Essentially, I didn't want someone who I had to deal with. I wanted someone who wanted to marry me, be married to only me, and be my forever date and we would date one another. This was only a portion of my boundaries. I wrote down some really graphical stuff and I went straight to God with it. I wanted a date worth keeping. I read this book by Henry Cloud, Ph.D. This book is so amazing. One thing for sure is that it works. What I love most is that there were no gimmicks, no tricks, no foolishness. Just trusting in God and in the process learning who I am and choosing eminent healing. The process was meant to make you. It was designed to make you into a better you for His glory. 1 Peter 5:10 (NIV) And the God of all grace, who called you to his eternal glory in Christ, after you have suffered a little while, will himself restore you and make you strong, firm and steadfast. In other words, God will restore you. However, there is always work to do, which is the process. Always appreciate the process. It is never pretty but it is imperative that we go through it to get to the crown of beauty that will be exchanged for ashes (Reynolds, 2018).

How this unfolded for me was in the recognition of the work that I did to improve myself for myself and ultimately, for the glory of God. I established boundaries that I refused to bend on. I established my 80/20 Rule and refused to bend on it. I recognized that my relationships suffered because I never knew how to be in a relationship. My relationships suffered because my parents didn't know how to teach me to be in a relationship. They didn't have it within themselves to give me. Instead of focusing on what I didn't have or get from my parents, which was a lot, I chose to focus on what I can obtain for myself. A lot of my life skills suffered for lack of knowledge. Hosea 4:6 (ESV) My people are destroyed for lack of knowledge. Because you have rejected knowledge, I reject you from being a priest to me. And since you have forgotten the law of your God, I also will forget your children. I was suffering. God blessed me with two sisters from other mothers and other misters. They are my unbiological sisters. They poured into me heavily. They gave me information that will forever be embedded in my mind. Although the devil meant for these situations to break me, God sought to turn it around for my good. Genesis 50:20 (NIV) You intended to harm me, but God intended it for good to accomplish what is now being done, the saving of many lives. We are presented with many opportunities in life. It is up to us to accept or reject the opportunity. Sometimes we take these opportunities and get the best prize out of it. Other times we take these chances and they turn out bad, dangerous and in some cases with a loss of life. I urge you more than anything else, put God's work first and do what He wants you to do to enhance His kingdom. Then the other things will be yours as well, Matthew 6:33 (CEV). Choose wisely in whatever you do.

That Social Media Post

The next time we communicated was on November 7th, 2010. Jerome Reynolds eventually gets into the conversation.

Jerome Reynolds: Y can't the educated woman with the pretty toes want her man to be the mill worker?"

Gaw'ga Peechy Keen: I don't have a problem with my man being a mill worker... not at all! Actually, I would prefer someone that is classy no matter what his job is as long as he knows how to be the head of the household and doesn't feel incompetent because of my educational background. Believe me, I know the struggles of life and would love to have someone that is more simplistic than myself to come home to.

Jerome Reynolds: That's what's up

Gaw'ga Peechy Keen: Oh and let me add... I wasn't born with a silver spoon in my mouth but together I figure that the two of us can make as many platinum spoons that we want!

Gaw'ga Peechy Keen: Until I get that man... the man that has me on his mind and the man that will cater to me (and God only knows what he will have waiting for him and I do have references – my unbiological sisters and my close friends who know my heart), then I am riding solo! COMPLETELY!

Jerome Reynolds: Just in case I never told u I'm simplistic and I work at a mill.

Gaw'ga Peechy Keen: LOL! You are too cute! lol

Jerome Reynolds: awww u makin me blush.

This conversation was crazy but it was amazing. He was very persistent, but very pleasant and was always a gentleman. Two of my friends kept asking me who he is. I had no clue. As they pressed me to find out, he kept liking all of my posts. One friend said, "Girl, you better find out who he is. He could be your husband. He is all over your posts." I answered saying, "Girl, he might be some stalker. He probably has a gang of baby mommas with a mouth full of gold teeth. He is probably a skirt chaser. He probably is trying to add another notch to his belt. He won't be doing that with me." She put the pressure on me to find out at least.

I really wasn't interested. The conversation was cool on social media. In my mind, he was in Georgia and I was in California. Therefore, this wasn't going to work. One of us had to give up our location. I always knew that I wanted to move back to Georgia, which is why I started planning my move. I didn't have a man on my mind though. I wasn't sure when, even though I had already started making plans. I had given myself 18 months to two years to make it happen. I was coming back as a property owner and I was going to have my BMW 745i. I had no clue how it was all going to happen. I just knew that it would with all of the work that I put in on myself and the faith that I had in God. My personal territory was bound to enlarge.

The Private Message
Later in the evening, I received a private message from him. The conversation went like this:

Him: He sent a photo of my toes.
Me: So do you know "THIS LADY?" (This lady was someone who I was friends with on Facebook)
Him: No.
Me: But how do you know her?
Him: From your page?

Me: So you asked her for her friendship?
Him: Yeah. Like 2 days ago.

Me: Hummm... okay!

my friend's list and add my friends. This is a serious pet peeve for This was a complete turn off for me I cannot stand for someone to browse me.

Him: Y what's up?
Me: I just wanted to know. I mean you're not my man so it's not like I have a right to say anything against it. But I am bothered by it.
Him: Really? I'm lost.
Me: It's no need to be lost and I guess it's something that I am dealing with. Anyway, she is a really nice lady.

I was thoroughly confused and started feeling like what I told my friend might be true. He just might be skirt chasing. He didn't need to be friends with my friends.

Him: I wouldn't know. Since she was your friend I figured she was ok.
Me: I guess it is since we are not dating or anything.
Him: But if we were it would be all about you.
Me: Why would you say that?
Him: I'm a one woman man so of course it would be about you.
Me: I am kinda digging this emotional connection. I guess I got scared a little bit when I saw that we had this person in common.
Him: I'll delete her if you want me too.
Me: That would be up to you.
Him: Ok
Me: I would rather you make that decision.
Him: I've already made it.
Me: Okay... whatever your decision is I respect it!
Him: She's gone. So I guess it's like Toni Tony Tone
Me: What do you mean about the 3 T's?
Him: Just me and u lol

Me: lol... that is sweet. So how tall are you Jerome?
Him: About 6'2".
Me: Okay!

In my mind, I was jumping for joy. He had one of the qualities that I needed. Height is essential for me.

Him: Y the exclamation point?

Me: lol... nice

Him: Yeah it has its advantages.

Me: Idk about the advantages but I don't like no short scrawny man.

Him: See. I have an advantage over a short and scrawny man. lol

Me: hahah! Gotcha!

Him: What u mean gotcha?

Me: Nice advantages.

Him: I know right! Yeah being tall has advantages.

Me: Well I am far from being tall.

Him: How tall are u?

Me: 5'2".

Him: You're right... not tall at all.

Everyone who knows me knows that I am short. This was something that I settled for and compromised in my last situationship. He was shorter than me. This was something that I WAS NOT bending on. As long as Jerome was taller than me with heels on I would have been fine with his height. With heels on, I was taller than the ex.

Me: Nope... lol. What are you doing?

Him: Chillin' at work. What are you doing?

Me: Waiting on my daughter to bring me my food.

Him: What's for dinner?

Me: Leftovers from last night from my book preview: baked chicken masala, dressing and vegi's!

Him: Sounds good.

Me: Thank you! It is good and I am starved. So do you talk to anyone else like you talk to me?

Him: No.

Me: So how do you know my cousin Jenee`?

Him: What about you?

Me: No I am not.

Him: Awwww. Now I feel special.

86

Me: lol! Other guys flirt but I am not into them. And I definitely haven't told anyone that I was digging an emotional connection. So tell me how you know my cousin. Did y'all used to date? Or are you selectively answering me?

Him: So are you into me??

Me: Idk I can't get an answer to my question? (The question was asking him how he knew my cousin Jenee').

Him: Who is your cousin?

Me: Jenee` Harris.

Him: Na I went to school with Jenee`

Me: what about the other lady?

Him: I don't know her.

Me: Okay... I just don't want to be talking to someone's ex that I know. I see that you know (unnamed)! I went to college with him when I lived in Brunswick. I'm surprised he hasn't been talking to me lately. Lol... he is cool peeps!

Him: Yeah. I worked with him for a lil while.

Me: So tell me about Mr. Simplistic. Why are you single with no children?

Him: I guess because I haven't found the right situation.

Me: What is the right situation?

Him: Have you ever thought about calling me?

Me: Have you ever thought about asking me to call you? Or, how about have you ever thought about calling me?

Him: What's the number?

Me: Wait a minute... where is the gentle Jerome teddy bear that has been talking to me on my wall for the longest? Who are you and is this how you ask a lady for her number?

Him: Oh. My bad. Would you be so kind as to bless me with your number please?

Me: lol! I didn't mean that formal... but yes.

If he had dated my cousin, he was definitely not going to get my phone number. That is girl code. When he confirmed that they hadn't I was ready for the phone conversation. I wondered what the sound and tone of his voice was like. If he sounded anything like Mike Tyson, this whole conversation would have been done. I would have been laughing too hard to talk. I know that he would have hung the phone up in my face.

Remembering My Boundaries
My boundaries consisted of
1. Matthew 6:33 (ISV) But first be concerned about God's kingdom and his righteousness, and all of these things will be provided for you as well.
2. Wisdom Proverbs 16:9; Proverbs 1:23, Proverbs 2:1-6
3. Being honest enough with myself to see and take everything at face value
4. Choosing not to get involved when I see that the seasons of life are different for the both of us
5. Accepting what is and not hang in there just because it is something that I wanted
6. I had to let go of the fear of losing for the reality of the inevitable
7. Learning to say NO and mean it
8. Refusing to settle for what is not for me
9. Refusing to compromise on what is not for me
10. Giving God my specifics, writing them on paper and making my vision plain with 80% of what I refuse to negotiate in a relationship/marriage and 20% of what I will negotiate on. When I wrote the vision and made it plain, according the Habakkuk 2:2-3, I gave God some graphical details that I absolutely preferred in my spouse.

The 80/20 Rule

The 80/20 Rule is simple. Eighty percent of my desires in a man was not negotiable under any circumstances. Twenty percent was negotiable. This is how I determined what I had to have and what I could live without. I established this for myself because we are not
perfect. There are many things that comprise an individual. However, there many things that we want to comprise an individual and they may not possess some of these things.

80% MUST HAVES
Man of God
Single AND Attainable
Feasible employment
His own house
His own car
Be a provider
Tall
Decent to look at
Willing to love me with his whole heart
Man of Integrity
Character
Loyal
Trustworthy
Reliability
Man of his word
Couldn't be insensitive
Affectionate
Soft hands and feet
And so on...

20% NEGOTIABLES
If he were fat, he could lose weight
If he were going bald, he could shave his head
If he had bad teeth, he could buy new ones
And so on...

I knew what I had to bring to the table. I needed to make sure that I knew what he was bringing to the table. Thus, I became who I wanted. So for the ladies who don't want to change because you're not going to change for no man, just know that you are attracting who you currently are. 2 Chronicles 7:14 (ERV) tell us: and if my people who are

called by my name become humble and pray, and look for me, and turn away from their evil ways, then I will hear them from heaven. I will forgive their sin and heal their land. I needed God to heal my land. I had to repent. I needed the change. I was not afraid to tell God that I needed Him. There is no other way. My pursuit for eminent change and healing didn't stop here. It is a process. I didn't care what I had to do to get there, I was going to do it. I committed to the process. I know that my Crown of Beauty had to be amazing because of all the storms that I weathered and all of the tears that I cried in my lifetime behind having a broken heart. Along with this came diagnoses of Major Depressive Disorder and Post Traumatic Stress Disorder and suicide ideation. Although I never had a plan to end my life, I felt worthless. I never felt affirmed by either of my parents. I had to forgive them as well. I had to forgive my dad over and over and over again because I got angry with him in the beginning of this process. I realized it no longer mattered because nothing can ever come of that situation. He left me. He confessed how horrible that he had been to me over the years. Regardless, I was still in my pursuit. Knowing that God said that He would never leave me nor forsake me, I clung tight to Him. Nonetheless, my 80/20 Rule worked for me.

THE PHONE CALL

It was so beautiful after he asked for my phone number. I was so intrigued when I answered the phone and heard his voice. The tone was perfect, and his voice is deep and sexy. At that moment, I wanted to know more. The conversation was soft and gentle in the beginning. When I discovered that he knew how to make me laugh and kept me going, I embraced and enjoyed the conversation. We talk for approximately 10 hours. We stayed on the phone talking and getting to know one another. Although I was still skeptical about doing this long-distance thing, I enjoyed that time talking to him. It was

refreshing. We were covering some serious ground. We talked about everything from why he doesn't have children and never gotten married to the 80/20 Rule and a few things about me. One of the things that I was cautious with was giving him too much information about things that happened to me in my past. I tried this before, and

it blew up in my face, and it was used against me.

After doing all of the work that I did on myself, I wasn't so trusting with my personal information straight upfront. I needed to take some time to get to know him and know that I can trust him. After all, isn't he, the man who is in the club and skirt-chasing with all the baby mamas? LOL! Once I found out that he was different from the way that I profiled him, I had to ask God to forgive me for judging a book by its cover. He seems like a cool guy thus far, but it's only one conversation. He called me the next day and wanted to know how I was doing. That conversation not only went well but turned into a lot more time that we spent on the phone. One of the things that I wanted to see is consistency. Even though I didn't list It in my 80/20 Rules, it is a part of what I needed. When he said that he was going to call back, he kept his word. Does that mean anything within two conversations? It can. For me, it did. It wasn't very often that he would have to call me back, but there were some occasions where he would. When he would tell me that he was going to call back, he did just that, and it wasn't light years later.

I was digging this conversation and how we connected. We covered so much ground within 48 hours that we decided to be in a relationship. He asked me to be his lady. I was extremely comfortable with him and I knew that I wanted him in my life. Throughout the conversations at various times, he would say, "There are some things that you just know." Although it was really peculiar, I was enjoying it. My friends kept asking me what I found out about this guy. When I changed my relationship status, that said it all. When he and I were on the phone, I could hear the beeps coming through my phone continuously. I kept on talking as though the beeps weren't coming through. I am smiling while I am typing this part because it was so astonishing how it unfolded. It was very unusual, non-traditional, and unconventional the way our relationship started. Little did I know the journey that I was on would be so amazing.

We discussed my first visit to come and spend time with him. I prepared to purchase my tickets to visit him. After I paid my bills for that month and paid my rent, I ran short on some money. He paid for everything that I couldn't so that I could get there to see him. I could not believe how this was flowing. It was a true breath of fresh air to have someone keep their word. Somewhere in my mind, I reflected about how I profiled him. Even though we were talking every day and phone dating, somewhere in there, I thought about him being a serial killer. Some serial killers go years without getting caught. I made sure all of the important people in my life who lived in California and Georgia knew about my upcoming visit. I gave them his information and where I was going to be in the event of any emergency. They had his address and his phone number. I made sure that I knew where the police station was. Regardless of the fact, you cannot be too careful when dating and trying to protect yourself. There was a time when I had been a victim to a violent crime, and I swore that I would never get in a vehicle with someone who I didn't know and trust. It was something about him that I couldn't quite put my finger on. He made me feel so comfortable. He was very consistent across all channels. I took a chance. In the mind of many, this could have been the stupidest thing ever. In the mind of those who take calculated risk, this could be considered one of the best choices ever. Regardless of what anyone's opinion is, this worked for me. I thought about the last relationship that I was in and how I felt on edge all the time. I thought about the relationship before that and relationship where my baby's father before he was brutally murdered. I was always on edge about something because there were so many unknown variables. With this man, everything was the opposite. When I felt comfortable enough to call him, he would answer. I rarely got a voicemail. If he missed my call, it was only moments that went by before he called me back. This man was amazing. I was ecstatic and excited about taking my trip to Georgia. We planned out the whole weekend. It was a time for me to get away and enjoy myself. I love the fact that whatever he said that he was going to do, he accomplished.

The day came for me to take my trip to Georgia. It was November 26th, 2010, the day after Thanksgiving. I arrived in Georgia later that

evening. We had no problem finding each other. When I laid eyes on him I couldn't help but remember a prophesy that I received in 2001 from a friend of mine. She said, "The Holy Spirit just showed me your husband. He is tall, dark skinned and he is driving a truck. He got out of the truck to open the door for you. I can't see his face, but I can see that he is your husband." The more unique thing about this is that I had dreams of a man and myself at the altar. He was tall and dark skinned. I could never see his face though. He was fresh out of high school in 2001. He was only 18 years old. I was 30 years old. That's right... he is younger than me. His face wasn't revealed because he wasn't ready for me.

Nonetheless, after spending the time that we did on the phone and seeing him in person, as well as knowing his age, it was suddenly clear. I knew why I couldn't see his face. Even though some things were starting to be clear, I didn't give myself permission to express it. I waited and held on to it for a long time.

During the weekend visit, he took me to dinner. He was a complete gentleman. Chivalry was not dead. I loved having my car door opened for me. I enjoyed having the restaurant doors held open for me. I especially enjoyed looking into his eyes, watching him eat and listening to him talk. I remember when my dad's wife said that she loved watching my dad eat. I thought that was so crazy until I experienced it myself. We went to visit a few of my friends and family and we picked up my son and godson. The setting was almost perfect. It was as though we were already a family. I couldn't wait to meet his family and know where he came from. I felt like the time would come soon enough. My family liked him. They kept asking, "Are you sure that he is from Brunswick?" They had never seen him around. Nonetheless, the weekend was a time well spent. I was able to sleep in and embrace a real winter. That is one of the things that I missed when I left Georgia to move back home to California. I was able to wear my boots and my big coat.

Sunday came too fast. I told him that I wanted to cook him dinner before I left. We went to the store to buy food. I put the meat in the oven. I washed my clothes and packed what was left. I packed enough stuff to stay for a week. You know how we are as women. I always need options when it comes to my clothes and shoes. I cooked country style ribs, fried cabbage, and cornbread. I was sad that he was left to eat alone. My departure was at hand. We had another good conversation on the way to the airport. He took care of everything. He walked me all the way to TSA. He held my hand as if he didn't want to let go. He leaned in to kiss me. He leaned in with another kiss. There it was... totally unexpected. He had a tear roll down his cheek. I was in shock. No man has ever shed a tear for me. It was a moment like no other. I had to move out of the way because others needed to get through TSA and was early. I had a few extra minutes to spare. I asked, "Is that a tear? Are you crying?" He responded in his cool voice, "A little bit." I wiped his tear, gave him a hug, and softly kissed his cheek. He asked, "Are you going to come back to see me?" I was hoping that I would have an invitation to return. I wasn't going to ask. I said, "Yes. If you want me to return, I will." He confirmed that he wanted me to return and that was all of the time that I had left. I had to get on the plane. "Will you call me when you land in Houston?" he asked. I told him that I would.

I boarded the plane and I found my seat. A cute little doggie jumped on my lap. His owner said, "He must really like you because he doesn't go to anyone." I smiled and quickly turned my head. The dog kept getting in my lap and I let him. By the time the lady tried to get him out of my lap again, I turned around bawling at the eyes. That last moment that I spent with him was sentimental. I had never felt anything like it. I have never connected with a man on this level. It was a feeling that is so indescribable. I knew in my heart that I wanted more.

When the woman seen my face, she asked, "Oh my goodness are you okay?" I nodded my head yes. I told her that I missed my boyfriend. She asked a few more questions. I can't even remember how I answered her. The plane took off and I tried to get my mind off of him. I tried to read and couldn't concentrate. We finally landed in Houston, Texas, on a layover. I took a quick bathroom break and grabbed a bite to eat and called him. I was so happy to hear his voice again. He expressed how he missed me already. I expressed the same affection. We talked for approximately 30 minutes before it was time for me to board the plane again. He asked me to let him know when I arrived at my car at LAX. By this time in my life, I was very comfortable in my skin. I did something that was indeed against every rule according those who play the game of love. I sent him a text message. The text message read:

"I have to tell you something. I have to tell you how I feel. I totally own what I am about to say and I understand if you are not there. I want to tell you that I love you."

I shut the phone down and got on the plane. My anxiety level was slightly high. I fell asleep until I arrived at LAX. You already know the first thing I did when I turned my phone on. I was looking for the response to my text message. There was nothing. My heart dropped. I thought to myself, "Well, I own my feelings and he is not required to reciprocate any feelings or emotions. You got this girl. Grab your bags and go to your car and call him to let him know that you made it and leave it at that." That is exactly what I did. I took a chance. I called him while my car was cooling off. It was winter in Georgia and Winter-Summer in California. LOL! He answered on the first ring. I let him know that I made it safely and that I was about to get in my car and thanked him for an awesome weekend and for being a total gentleman. Just as I was about to hang the phone up, he said, "I have to tell you that I feel the exact same way. I love you too." My heart was dancing. He road home with me on the phone and our phone dating started up again. I had a long ride and the conversation was lovely and pleasant. After arriving home, I took a shower to get all of the airport and airplane off of me so that I could relax comfortably.

Meanwhile, Back in Cali...

I couldn't help but to thank God. I put in some work on myself. The flow of love was truly in the air. I called my girls to catch up with them. It wasn't long before I was back on the phone with him again. This time he had something that he needed to ask me. He said, "I am really feeling you and our relationship, even though everything is brand new. I am in this for the long haul. I only have one request. If you see me falling, will you hold my hand until I get through it?" I said, "Yes. Yes I will." It was becoming clear that the trauma that I endured in the past was well with me. He blessed me to have triumph over tragedy.

As with anything in life, we can all cry woe is me. Ruth could have mourned the death of her husband longer than we can imagine. Instead, she inhabited the concept of taking care of her mother in love. She made sure to take care of her needs by gleaning in a particular field. The meeting of Ruth and Boaz in his field emphasizes the role of God's providence in looking after the needs of the two widows. Later, when Boaz blessed Ruth, Naomi recognized Boaz's dedication to them as family (2:20) and advised Ruth to continue gleaning in Boaz's fields because he had guaranteed her safety (2:22) (Zondervan, 1994, 2003, 2011).. She might have had her tearful moments because it's what happens with human emotions. However, she kept pushing through. Although our circumstances that surround our situations do not mirror in totality, the strength to press on does. I never had an opportunity to sit and cry over my situation. Being an unwanted child caused me to have to always find a way. All things considered; rejection wasn't my best friend. By the time I might have considered crying, I had already evolved to a new level in my life. I reflected on the challenges that surfaced between my ex-boyfriend and me. It was a pivotal breaking point that sparked me to choose to change or stay in the same place. It was the straw that broke the camel's back. In previous relationships, whether it was dating or serious, when I sensed that things were broken, I swiftly ended it, and moved on with my business, that is, until I met Mr. Dressed Up In Lies. My settlement radar was extremely high. As I purposefully moved forward with my plans for
healing, I refused to stop until I accomplished a goal of being complete. I didn't have time to focus on the downtrodden chain of events that encircled the disintegration of the relationship with Mr. Love Pistol.

Whether the goal is to find a new job, another car, new apartment, buy a home, start a business or rebuilding your current
relationship/marriage, you have to move out of your head and into the work that needs to be done in order for you to overcome all of the encounters that facilitated your choices to get to this point. Your encounters can be emotional, physical, and/or mental. The timing of overcoming depends on how you process your challenges. I didn't have a lot of time between life's challenges to process before having to make a move. By the time I was able to settle into a new situation, I found myself giving God the praise and the glory. John 14:27 (NIV) says Peace I leave with you; my peace I give you. I

do not give to you as the world gives. Do not let your hearts be troubled and do not be afraid. I never had time to really be afraid. I had to make whatever power moves that were necessary for my children and me. Therefore, sitting and wailing in your troubles will not help you to get things moving.

Decree & Declare:
Think about situations where you felt like you were rejected, neglected, and abandoned. Remember how you felt. Take some time to praise and thank God for seeing you through these situations.
See what God says about you.

Pick one to decree and declare over yourself each day. Although there are only 16 listed, you can find more scriptures and do your own research. If God didn't believe in you, he would not have called you. He would not care about the number of hairs on your head. Luke 12:7 (TLB) And he knows the number of hairs on your head! Never fear, you are far more valuable to him than a whole flock of sparrows. Will you choose to let God have His way? Will you say YES to His will? Will you be among the chosen?

"Therefore, if anyone is in Christ, he is a new creation. The old has gone, the new has come."
2 Cor. 5:17

"All this is from God, who reconciled us to himself through Christ and gave us the ministry of reconciliation: that God was reconciling the world to himself in Christ, not counting people's sins against them. And he has committed to us the message of reconciliation." 2 Cor 5:18-19
"And to put on the new self, created to be like God in true righteousness and holiness." Ephesians 4:24

Jesus answered, "Very truly I tell you, no one can enter the kingdom of God unless they are born of water and the Spirit. Flesh gives birth to flesh, but the Spirit[b] gives birth to spirit. John 3:3-6

"God saved you by his grace when you believed. And you can't take credit for this; it is a gift from God." Ephesians 2:8

"You are the light of the world. A town built on a hill cannot be hidden." Matthew 5:14

"Then you will shine among them like stars in the sky." Philippians 2:15

"You are all children of the light and children of the day. We do not belong to the night or to the darkness."1 Thessalonians 5:5

"You are the salt of the earth." Matthew 5:13

"For God, who said, "Let light shine out of darkness," made his light shine in our hearts to give us the light of the knowledge of God's glory displayed in the face of Christ." 2 Corinthians 4:6

"Light shines on the godly, and joy on those whose hearts are right." Psalm 97:11
When you realize your self-worth, beauty, and joy in Christ, you have the fearlessness to step into your destiny and Reign...

"No, in all these things we are more than conquerors through him who loved us." Romans 8:37

"Therefore, holy brothers and sisters, who share in the heavenly calling, fix your thoughts on Jesus, whom we acknowledge as our apostle and high priest." Hebrews 3:1

"But you are a chosen people, a royal priesthood, a holy nation, God's special possession, that you may declare the praises of him who called you out of darkness into his wonderful light." 1 Peter 2:9

"For we are God's handiwork, created in Christ Jesus to do good works, which God prepared in advance for us to do." Ephesians 2:10

"Now if we are children, then we are heirs- heirs of God and co-heirs with Christ. If indeed we share in His sufferings in order that we may also share with His glory." Romans 8:17

"You did not choose me, but I chose you and appointed you so that you might go and bear fruit—fruit that will last—and so that whatever you ask in my name the Father will give you." John 15:16

Even though you are able to think about what others may feel or think about you, what is more important is the way that God feels about you. Once you can embrace it you can move into eminent healing and make necessary changes for yourself. You will be able to make changes that heal you internally so that you will radiate with the glow of Jesus. John 8:12 (AMPC) says Once more Jesus addressed the crowd. He said, I am the Light of the world. He who follows Me will not be walking in the dark, but will have the Light which is Life.

<u>Tenets of Faith</u>

1.   Nothing will change unless you change it. God is not going to drop this dramatic change from heaven into your lap. If that is the case, He would have already did for you and everyone. We have to open the door of our hearts for Him to come in.

James 2:14-26 (ESV)

Faith Without Works Is Dead

What good is it, my brothers, if someone says he has faith but does not have works? Can that faith save him? If a brother or sister is poorly clothed and lacking in daily food, and one of you says to them, "Go in peace, be warmed and filled," without giving them the things needed for the body, what good is that? So also faith by itself if it does not

have works, is dead.

Read the remainder of this passage: verses James 2:18 – 26

2.   Understand that God is not going to drop your mate from heaven. The husband that you desire is already here. If he is in heaven, that means that he is not yours and he belongs solely to the Lord and he will not be returning to earth to marry you. Think about the presentation that took place between Ruth and Boaz. The bible calls him a worthy man. Ruth was busy in the field to gather leftover grains after the harvest for her and Naomi to eat. Boaz was informed about the death of Ruth's husband and how she was taking care of her mother-in-love. Ruth found favor with Boaz.

He instructed those around her not to reprimand her, but to allow her to glean. Ruth was obedient. She followed instructions from Boaz and from Naomi. She was humble. Boaz called her a worthy woman. What happened between Ruth and Boaz was an opportunity. This is the key factor to moving into something. Thus, the Holy Spirit may present an opportunity. It is up to you to take the chance. God is not forcing you nor me to stay with anyone. We have to choose. Therefore, if you are a wife who is a victim of infidelity, have a husband who has not fully embraced his role as a husband, and even if you are dating, just know that it is your decision to stay. The Holy Spirit will give you wisdom on the why's of staying or leaving. Regardless, the opportunity is yours and so is the decision. DO NOT blame God as Adam did when he was caught in his sin saying, "It's the fault of the woman you put here with me. She gave me some fruit from the tree. And I ate it" Genesis 3:12 (NIRV). God is not the root of your fall or misunderstandings of His word. Nevertheless, when Boaz purchased the land and all the benefits of it, which Ruth was one of the benefits, he took Ruth as his wife.

Ruth 2, 3 and 4.
In my first marriage, my ex-husband wanted to be single and married. I wanted to be married. We were not in the same season of life and I made a decision to quit. You have to choose for you. No one can judge you. The choice is yours. If you choose to stay, pray and trust God to turn things around.

3.   You have to do something. Ruth did something. Abraham did something. If you notice that everything that you have tried is not working, your support system is null, or just can't seem to get things right or even if everything is perfect in your world, sometimes, God will instruct or present opportunities in other places. Sometimes, we may have an inkling of the opportunities. When we go on the instruction of the Holy Spirit, we are going with the trust in the Lord that the provision is made for the vision that He has given us. We have the promises of God but we do not always know the path that will take us there. We have to trust God.

Ruth 2:11 But Boaz answered her, "All that you have done for your mother-in-law since the death of your husband has been fully told to me, and how you left your father and mother and your native land and came to a people that you did not know before.

Genesis 12:1-4 The Lord had said to Abram, "Go from your country, your people and your father's family. Go to the land I will show you. "I will make you into a great nation. And I will bless you.
I will make your name great. You will be a blessing to others. I will bless those who bless you. I will put a curse on anyone who puts a curse on you. All nations on earth will be blessed because of you." So Abram went, just as the Lord had told him.

The difference is that Ruth made a choice and Abram was instructed. Whether you choose to or you are instructed to do something, God will make it for your good. You will see a VICTORY.

Distant Lovers

That is it... that old Marvin Gaye tune crept up in there. This was our scenario. I lived so many miles from him. With each day and time spent on the phone, we grew closer and closer. I was scheduled to have a procedure to correct some feminine issues. The plus was that I didn't want any more children and he was okay with not having any biological children. This was the first day that we didn't phone date. He checked on me regardless of the fact that I had to sleep off the anesthesia. The

next day we were back to our usual selves. It had gotten to the point where we would fall asleep and wake up on the phone. If he had to work, we texted all night until I fell asleep. When he got off work, we would talk until he fell asleep. It became a science. When he fell asleep, I would turn the volume down and get on my house phone and chop it up with my friends to catch up. No one ever knew that he was on another phone. When he would awaken, I would be right there for him to hear my voice.

We planned to skip our visit for December so that I could spend Christmas with my children as I normally did. Christmas 2010 was on a Saturday. I anticipated and planned to skip our phone date. It was December 23rd, 2010, my son's birthday again. I waited for his call. He texted. I called him. Even though he answered, he was short on words. Initially, I thought that he was avoiding me. He assured me that he was not avoiding me. He was at his parents' home and said that he doesn't feel good. He said, "It hurts when I talk." I gave him a few home remedies, such as making a hot toddy, drink warm tea without the toddy or take some throat lozenges. None of that worked. On Christmas Eve, I told him to go to the emergency room. It might be more serious than we think. Indeed it was. Unfortunately, he had to have an emergency outpatient surgery. During this time, our phone date was via text. We refused to let up. I felt so bad that I wasn't able to be there with him. A last minute flight was over $2000. At Christmas time for this single mother, I sincerely did not have it. I text him a prayer and told him that I was right there. We texted until approximately 3:00 am Pacific Standard Time. I got about four hours of sleep. I wanted to know how he was doing. I wanted to hear his voice. I texted him to let him know that I was awake. We texted until the surgery was complete. He was still groggy and wanted to sleep afterwards. I gave him my kind regards and looked forward to speaking to him again when he awakened.

He felt much better but he had a little bit of a recovery ahead of him. I apologized over and over for not being able to be there with him. He was understanding and didn't count it against me. The fact that I
stayed in contact with him while he was going through it is what made him happy. The next trip was already planned and paid for. This trip was for my birthday. We planned to go to Pelican Point in Darien, Georgia, for dinner and have a relaxing and enjoyable weekend. This time, I rented a car. I stopped to get my hair done upon my arrival. This was the second time that I was seeing him and he would have to see me with my hair in a scarf and rollers. LOL. He had to meet me at the convenient store because I wasn't familiar with my surroundings. He was so happy to see me and likewise, I was so happy to see him. He had just gotten off work. When he pulled up and got out of his truck, I saw the gleam in his eyes. He really missed me. For my birthday, I was given the key to his home. He said, "This key is for you to come and go as you please. You don't even have to let me know that you are coming down here. Just come whenever you feel. This is our home." I was shocked and happy all in the same breath. I had never had such access to something so big in my life. I felt like I was truly the center of his world. He let me know that everything that he was doing from that moment forward pertained to the development of the team of WE. What was so beautiful about this is that he showed me everything that he said. It was effortless for him.

The next day, I went shopping. I was preparing for our evening out. We double dated with my cousin and her husband. Dinner at Pelican Point was amazing. It was great company and an enjoyable time. My cousin and her husband loved him. She made sure to text me to let me know that she seen the gleam in his eyes. She was happy because she was the one who prayed for me when I was going through with the ex. One thing she said in that particular prayer was, "Father, please let my cousin have the kind of love that you blessed me with from my husband." BaeBaeh... I felt that. When she prayed that prayer it resonated deep in my spirit. I knew that I had love under new management with my Beau. She watched him in complete chivalry. If I moved, he moved. He was sure to show off his chivalrous manners. My cousin had me blushing.

I was able to visit with my family and friends spontaneously. I went shopping again. I was able to hang out a little bit before I left. Everyone else had so many questions and could not wait to meet him. I was equally excited and could not wait to introduce him to everyone. The time came for me to leave again. I already had my tickets to come back in February 2011. In the meantime and in between time we phone dated and I continued to visit him. It was truly a pleasure and a breath of fresh air because I knew that I wanted to move back to Georgia. I am always going to be a Cali girl, but I wanted to be back in Georgia. My heart never left.

Southeast Georgia is slower paced than California. It was serene. It became my home. It was the first time that I lived in one place longer than 2 years. My last residence in Compton was the first time that I lived in one place for longer than one year. My life was full of instability and nomadic activity. My new love wanted to give me everything that I never had. I didn't receive any of this from my first husband. Looking back, I realize that he didn't have it in him to be a Boaz type of husband. Although the breakup of my marriage hurt, I learned early on not to hate him. He gave all that he had in him, just like Mr. Dressed Up In Lies, Mr. Totally Ambivalent and Mr. Love Pistol. Have you ever found yourself saying, "Why can't he...?" "If he would just..." "How come he won't...?" Sis, let me tell you that it is a two way street. Either you have not lived up to your end of what you said you would no longer do or accept, you haven't demanded that certain level of reverence from him, you have settled and compromised, you have not done your work, or he just can't be all that you need him to be. He is not going to change anything unless he chooses to do so. He is not going to live up to the standards that you believe that he should. If you are married and one of these points is your scenario, prayer is your best ally. God can move on his heart and change him. However, be sure that you are working to change as well. Understandably, some men don't have relevant role models. Therefore, he can't give more than what is in him unless he is seeking to be a better person for himself first. There are some men who don't mind being taught. However, you have to make sure to treat him with the same respect that you feel that you deserve if it were you. We are all unlearned in many areas of life. Where we fall short, we have to be willing to learn in order to level up to a new degree of triumph. You can't demand what you aren't. You can't expect what you cannot give. Remember, the bible called Boaz a worthy man. Boaz called Ruth a worthy woman. In Ruth 3:11 (ESV), when Boaz says, "And now, my daughter, do not fear. I will do for you all that you ask, for all my fellow townsmen know that you are a worthy woman," he is referring to her as a woman of noble character. Ruth's presence commanded the atmosphere. Simply put, her virtue was pleasant, meek, bold, and fearless, yet she was a servant and did it with her whole heart.

We Closed the Gap

After all of my traveling back and forth, we knew that we definitely wanted to be together. He asked me to move back sooner than anticipated. My last visit in April 2011 was my final visit before my move back. I packed my things into storage. He sent me the money to purchase tickets for me and my two youngest daughters. We left California for good on May 4th, 2011. Georgia has been home ever since. My son was already here and my oldest daughter came shortly after. It was an adjustment, but it worked. There were no regrets from neither of us. We were in love and we wanted our relationship more than anything.

Returning to Georgia happened at the right time. I was ready to leave California behind. It was too expensive. It was too congested. There were so many people everywhere that I went. Mostly, it did not have my love there. Dating long distance is extremely difficult, especially when you want to spend every moment with the one you love. According to Long Distance Relationships:

- 14 million couples define themselves as having a long distance relationship
- 3.75 million married couples are in a long distance relationship
- 32.5 % of all long distance relationships are college relationships
- 75 % of all engaged couples have been (at some point) in a long distance relationship
- 2.9 % of all married couples in the states live in a long distance relationship
- 10 % of all marriages in the states started out as a long distance relationship

Other stats suggest:
- 4.5 months – the average time before a long distance relationship breaks down
- 40 % of all long distance relationships ends with a break-up
- 70 % of all failed long distance relationships fails due to unplanned changes

Yet, additional stats report:
- 125 miles – the average distance in long distance relationships
- 1.5 times – the average number of times couples visited each other (per month)
- 3 letters – the average number of letters couples write each other (per month)
- 2.7 days – the average number of days between couples calling each other
- 14 months – the average number of months before couples expect to move back together

(Guldner, 2008 – 2020).

We were determined not to fail at this relationship despite what the statistics say. I remember thinking that our relationship was doomed to fail. The thought of us making it was terrifying. Besides, I had never had a successful relationship. Why should this one be the one? He was everything that I wanted in a man. He treated me with the love and respect that I longed for. Most of all, we were in the same season of our lives and had the same goals for love and marriage. I remember attempting to sabotage our relationship by telling him that it isn't going to work. He asked me to come sit next to him. He asked, "What's going on? Why do you believe that we are not going to make it?" I answered, "None of my other relationships succeeded. I don't think that this one will either." As he was holding my hands, he gently squeezed them and said, "Look at it this way; none of my relationships succeeded before you either. They weren't meant to be. We are. I told you that I am in this for the long haul and I mean it. I want everything with you." Tears ran down my face. I was relieved. We prayed and thanked God for one another and for our marriage to come.

The first step had already been accomplished and that was moving back to Georgia to close the gap. We wanted to date on a regular basis. It was essential. It was pertinent. It was astounding to feel the love that I knew that I deserved. It was the love that I longed to give to someone deserving. Roughly two and a half years prior, my dad's wife said, "God will never bless you with a good man. You don't even know what a good man looks like." She said that at a time when I was dealing with some heavy issues with Mr. Totally Ambivalent. Mr. Totally Ambivalent is truly befitting of him. The only thing that he was consistent at was being ambivalent. Finally, I asked God for the strength to move on from this because apparently, he was not the one for me. She said this at a time when I was weak within myself. I had no blueprint to guide me. Apparently, my downfall was a mockery to her. She said it in such a manner that I could never be as privileged as her. She was married to my dad for 25 years before his demise. This too, was a lesson for me. As I sought to withdraw from her toxicity, I prepared to move on with my life in silence.

The lesson took me back to frenemies and the haughty spirit. The lesson mainly taught me to NEVER say what and who God will or will not ever bless. If your marriage is in turmoil, if you want it, seek God. If your relationship is in turmoil, seek God. He has the answers. He will lead you. Ultimately, He will give you the wisdom to move on if that is in His will. You have to be open to it and lean on His everlasting arm in the process. His strength is made perfect in our time of weakness. 2 Corinthians 12:9 (ESV) But he said to me, "My grace is sufficient for you, for my power is made perfect in weakness." Therefore I will boast all the more gladly of my weaknesses, so that the power of Christ may rest upon me.

Nonetheless, the supreme lesson is to be careful how and what you say about someone's situation. You never know if and when it can be you. You never know if it is the last thing that you say to a person that will push them over the edge, in the famous words of my dear sister from another mother and another mister. The one thing that someone does not need is to be kicked when they're already down. Therefore, hearing my Boo say those words to me gave me comfort and calmed my spirit. I was ready to marry him right then. LOL.

From Relationship to Engagement

Not long after my move back did I receive my engagement ring. Our engagement was sweet and simple but ever so unforgettable. The best part is that he let me choose my ring. He wanted me to have something that I loved and that I would wear long term. His ring was simple. We discussed having a big wedding, which is what I wanted. He asked me to have a simple wedding so that he can buy me a home that we both took time to choose. I was in love with the home that he gave me. It had its hidden jewels just for me. No other women had ever been inside or spent any time in it other than his mom and sister. He bought a brand new bed and furniture when he bought the house, which also meant that no other women had ever spent any time in that either. Not only did he adore me, but he kept himself for me. I used to hear women say that it is hard to keep a man. Or, having a piece of a man is better than having no man at all. Remember, my dad's stepdaughter tried to tell me that she could teach me how to keep a man. GIRL STOP. None of that was for me. If I am giving a whole me, I need a whole you.

I never needed anyone to teach me how to keep a man. I needed to know how to attract a man that knew how to keep himself. I needed a man who felt that I am worth saving himself for. She felt privy to approach me with that conversation because she dated a man for nearly a decade. However, our dynamics were very different. I refuse to be someone's girlfriend longer than two years. This is another boundary and 80/20 Rule. I don't have that kind of time to give anyone without nuptials. There were other major differences that turned me off about this conversation. She and her guy both lived at home with their mothers. She had never lived on her own and she was almost 40 years old. I required certain things from a man. My standards were relaxed in certain areas but living at home with his mother/father or both of his parents was not going to cut it for me. While I do not despise someone living at home, it wasn't something that was on my list of negotiables. I needed someone who knew about survival or at least was responsible with his finances and knew how to pay his bills outside of living with his parents. This is because I didn't have a home to go back to. Thus, he had to be on a greater level of accountability for me.

Therefore, I shut the whole conversation and idea down because it was not coming from a place of true compassion. I didn't need that haughty spirit trying to teach me anything. Proverbs 16:18 (KJV) Pride goeth before destruction, and an haughty spirit before a fall. Be careful who you allow to pour into you. Some people profess to be your friend but in actuality, they are frenemies. You have to know the difference. Do not be afraid to cut them off. They watch in jealousy and envy. You do not have to succumb to their demands for your life and journey. If you are not sure, ask your daddy, God to order your steps. Psalm 37:23 (KJV) The steps of a good man are ordered by the Lord: and he delighteth in his way. God plans and orders the pathways of the man who lives in fellowship with Him. He upholds the one whose ways please Him. Though such a man may fall into trials and tribulations, he will never be engulfed by them, for the Lord holds him securely by His hand. It is also true that if a righteous man falls into sin, he will not be abandoned by the Lord, though this is not the specific kind of fall that this verse is referring to (MacDonald, 1989-2016).

As time progressed, we were ready for our marriage. Many people felt like I was a hidden jewel. He didn't take me around anyone for some time. He was questioned by his family. I began to feel the same way. He met the important ones in my family but I hadn't met any of his. He had never taken anyone home to meet his parents. He never understood the reason behind meeting the family if I belonged to him. He figured whenever we could get together we would. He has such a cool, calm, and relaxed demeanor. It literally did not faze him. Not long after this discussion, we met one another. They liked me and I liked them. His mother wondered why I didn't get her number from his phone. I explained to her that I am not the type of woman to search through my man's phone. If he didn't give it to me, I didn't look for it.

Not only did I meet his parents and his sister, I met his aunts and a few of his cousins. I learned early on that he is definitely his father's child. The way that he has been with me is the same way that his father has been with his mother. They have been married for 40 plus years. They are a close family. They truly love their own and it shows. Nonetheless, they were happy for us. We set our wedding date. The fun began from there. I planned to do everything as budget friendly as possible. He was very non-traditional. He hated suits and dress clothes. I was not going to let that stop me. I was about to be his wife and I wanted to feel the moment. There was one element that was left out. He hadn't told his parents about our wedding day yet. I wanted to tell his mother and father. I asked him if he wanted me to tell them. He said that he would take care of it. He had his time when he wanted to tell them. When he did, I received a phone call from his mother. She wanted to know why I hadn't spilled the beans about our wedding. I said, "He wanted to tell you himself. I wasn't going to go over his head and say anything." I had to respect his time. This is his parents. I also felt that it sounded better coming from him. I could tell that she was in tears. She said, "Please don't hurt my baby. I know that he is a grown man, but please don't hurt him." I understood where she was coming from because they wanted to meet me and find out about me firsthand. I softly responded, "Ask God about me." I could have given her the run down about who I am and how I maneuver. However, the best one to ask is the one who created me.

When we spoke the next day, she said, "I asked God and He showed me your warm spirit." She wanted me to know and understand that marriage is until death. I explained with the swiftness, we are in this until death or the return of Christ. Either way, we chose to be all in.

Our Wedding Day

Christmas soon came and went. New Year's Eve was approaching faster than we could blink. I reserved a honeymoon suite at the Oceanside Inn and Suites on Jekyll Island. I checked in on the evening of December 30th. I set everything up for our special night. It had to be a night to remember. I was marrying the man who I was in love with. He was in love with me. His love started out as everything for me. I only hoped that I would have it for a lifetime.

On New Year's Eve I went to run a few last minute errands. I needed to get my nails done, which was the only thing that I wasn't going to do since I was a DIY bride. I knew the ceremony was going to be small, I didn't set up any decorations. I had a matron of honor, which was my cousin who went through the trenches with me. I had two bridesmaids, which was his sister and one of my other cousins. My sister wasn't able to be there. She texted me and had me feeling so princess like. She felt like I deserved this moment. She was overjoyed with my growth. I learned a great deal from her. I was happy, nervous, and felt complete within myself. I wouldn't have traded this moment for anything. We were pronounced husband and wife and we kissed like never before. I was in the moment. My stepfather and his wife took us out to dinner. We had a great time, but we were ready to get our own party started. When he finally had an opportunity to see the honeymoon suite and how I had it set up he was excited. the rest of the night was history. It was lovely. I married my Boaz.

As I am writing this book, I am reflecting on so many beautiful moments that we experienced. November 10th, 2020 will be 10 years that we have officially been together and New Year's Eve 2020 will be nine years of marriage. We still have forever to go. The level of being in love grows every day. If I could, I would marry him every day. My life with him has been nothing short of blissful. Have we had some hard days? Yes. Have we had some challenges? Yes. Most of them haven't been our own, but we still made it through and we are going strong.

Ladies, if you want your Boaz:
Believe in your desire. Remain
Optimistic throughout your process. Maintain an
Attitude of gratitude. Approach each day with
Zeal – you have to make some changes within you.

The changes are for you but others will reap the benefits. The changes are important for your own empowerment. They are mandatory in order for you to demand your respect. If you stay the same, nothing changes. If you change, then everything changes. While change is difficult to embrace at times, it can be a beautiful thing. Think of a butterfly and the process that it goes through to become its beautiful self. Embrace the change. It is eminent. You will love you even more. You have to make the change about you. You will never be the same and you will not regret it. In fact, you will see toxicity weeded out of your life. It will only return if you open the door. In closing, change is the beginning of something new and it is especially for you.

Personal SWOT Analysis

To retrieve your free copy of the Personal SWOT Analysis, visit
https://www.theruthfactor.org/shop
Enter Code: FREESWOT

REFERENCES

American College of Obstetricians and Gynecologists. Labor and delivery. In: Your Pregnancy and Childbirth Month to Month. 6th ed. Washington, D.C.: American College of Obstetricians and Gynecologists; 2015.

BibleGateway. (n.d.). Retrieved from https://www.biblegateway.com/passage/?search=1 Chronicles 4:9-10&version=NKJV

BibleGateway. (n.d.). Retrieved from https://www.biblegateway.com/passage/?search=2 Chronicles 7:14&version=ERV

BibleGateway. (n.d.). Retrieved from https://www.biblegateway.com/passage/?search=1 Corinthians 13:4-8&version=AMP

BibleGateway. (n.d.). Retrieved from https://www.biblegateway.com/passage/?search=2 Corinthians 12:9&version=AMPC

BibleGateway. (n.d.). Retrieved from https://www.biblegateway.com/passage/?search=2 Corinthians 12:9&version=ESV

BibleGateway. (n.d.). Retrieved from
https://www.biblegateway.com/passage/?search=Deuteronomy
31:6&version=AMPC

BibleGateway. (n.d.). Retrieved from
https://www.biblegateway.com/passage/?search=Genesis
12:1&version=NKJV

BibleGateway. (n.d.). Retrieved from
https://www.biblegateway.com/passage/?search=Genesis
3&version=NIRV

BibleGateway. (n.d.). Retrieved from
https://www.biblegateway.com/passage/?search=Genesis
50:20&version=NIV

BibleGateway. (n.d.). Retrieved from
https://www.biblegateway.com/passage/?search=Habakkuk
1&version=NKJV

BibleGateway. (n.d.). Retrieved from
https://www.biblegateway.com/passage/?search=Hosea
4:6&version=ESV

BibleGateway. (n.d.). Retrieved from
https://www.biblegateway.com/passage/?search=Isaiah
41:10&version=ESV

BibleGateway. (n.d.). Retrieved from
https://www.biblegateway.com/passage/?search=Isaiah
61:3&version=ESV

BibleGateway. (n.d.). Retrieved from
https://www.biblegateway.com/passage/?search=james
1:2&version=NLT

BibleGateway. (n.d.). Retrieved from
https://www.biblegateway.com/passage/?search=Jeremiah
29:11&version=AMPC

BibleGateway. (n.d.). Retrieved from
https://www.biblegateway.com/passage/?search=John
8:12&version=AMPC

BibleGateway. (n.d.). Retrieved from
https://www.biblegateway.com/passage/?search=John
14:27&version=NIV

BibleGateway. (n.d.). Retrieved from
https://www.biblegateway.com/passage/?search=jonah1&version
=NKJV

BibleGateway. (n.d.). Retrieved from
https://www.biblegateway.com/passage/?search=Luke
12:7&version=TLB

BibleGateway. (n.d.). Retrieved from
https://www.biblegateway.com/passage/?search=Matthew
6:33&version=CEV

BibleGateway. (n.d.). Retrieved from
https://www.biblegateway.com/passage/?search=Matthew
6:33&version=ISV

BibleGateway. (n.d.). Retrieved from
https://www.biblegateway.com/passage/?search=1 Peter
5:10&version=NIV

BibleGateway. (n.d.). Retrieved from
https://www.biblegateway.com/passage/?search=2 Peter
3:18&version=NKJV

BibleGateway. (n.d.). Retrieved from
> https://www.biblegateway.com/passage/?search=Proverbs
> 11:14&version=CEB

BibleGateway. (n.d.). Retrieved from
> https://www.biblegateway.com/passage/?search=Proverbs
> 16:18&version=KJV

BibleGateway. (n.d.). Retrieved from
> https://www.biblegateway.com/passage/?search=proverbs
> 4:7&version=NKJV

BibleGateway. (n.d.). Retrieved from
> https://www.biblegateway.com/passage/?search=Proverbs
> 16:9&version=NKJV

BibleGateway. (n.d.). Retrieved from
> https://www.biblegateway.com/passage/?search=Proverbs
> 16:9&version=TLB

BibleGateway. (n.d.). Retrieved from
> https://www.biblegateway.com/passage/?search=Psalm
> 37:23&version=KJV

BibleGateway. (n.d.). Retrieved from
> https://www.biblegateway.com/passage/?search=Psalm 51:17
> &version=NIV

BibleGateway. (n.d.). Retrieved from
> https://www.biblegateway.com/passage/?search=Romans
> 9:17&version=NKJV

BibleGateway. (n.d.). Retrieved from
> https://www.biblegateway.com/passage/?search=Romans
> 12:2&version=NIV

BibleGateway. (n.d.). Retrieved from

      https://www.biblegateway.com/passage/?search=2 Timothy

      1:7&version=CEV

"BibleGateway - Emotional Self-care." Philippians 4:8 KJV - - Bible

      Gateway. Accessed July 03, 2020.

      https://www.biblegateway.com/passage/?search=Philippians

      4:8&version=KJV.

BibleGateway - Intellectual. (n.d.). Retrieved from

      https://www.biblegateway.com/passage/?search=Luke

      12:48&version=NKJV

BibleGateway - Occupational. (n.d.). Retrieved from

      https://www.biblegateway.com/passage/?search= Colossians

      3:23&version=ESV

BibleGateway - Physical Self-care. (n.d.). Retrieved from

      https://www.biblegateway.com/passage/?search=1 Corinthians

      3:16-17&version=NKJV

BibleGateway - Psychological Self-care. (n.d.). Retrieved from

      https://www.biblegateway.com/passage/?search=Proverbs

      11:14&version=NKJV

BibleGateway - Social. (n.d.). Retrieved from

      https://www.biblegateway.com/passage/?search=John 13:34-

      35&version=ESV

BibleGateway - Spiritual. (n.d.). Retrieved from

      https://www.biblegateway.com/passage/?search=Joshua

      1:8&version=AMP

BibleGateway - Tenets of Truth. (n.d.). Retrieved from
https://www.biblegateway.com/passage/?search=2 Corinthians
6:14 &version=AMPC

BibleGateway - Tenets of Truth. (n.d.). Retrieved from
https://www.biblegateway.com/passage/?search=Hebrews
10:26&version=ESV

BibleGateway - Tenets of Truth. (n.d.). Retrieved from
https://www.biblegateway.com/passage/?search=Mark 6:31-
32&version=TLB

BibleGateway - Tenets of Truth. (n.d.). Retrieved from
https://www.biblegateway.com/passage/?search=Proverbs 12:19
&version=NIV

BibleGateway - Tenets of Truth. (n.d.). Retrieved from
https://www.biblegateway.com/passage/?search=Proverbs
16:18&version=CEB

Boaz called Ruth a Worthy Woman. (2019). Retrieved from
https://www.biblegateway.com/passage/?search=Ruth
3&version=ESVNIV Biblical Theology Study Bible

Collingwood, J. (2018). The Importance of Personal Boundaries. Retrieved
from https://psychcentral.com/lib/the-importance-of-personal-
boundaries/

Crampton, L. (2020). Roses: Plant and Flower Facts, Photos, and Symbolic
Meanings. Retrieved from https://owlcation.com/stem/Roses-
Symbols-of-Love-and-Flowers-of-Beauty

Cunningham FG, et al. Normal labor. In: Williams Obstetrics. 24th ed. New
York, N.Y.: The McGraw-Hill Companies; 2014.
http://www.accessmedicine.com. Accessed June 16, 2016.

Farlex Dictionary of Idioms. (2015). Chase Your Tail. Retrieved April 21,
2020 from https://idioms.thefreedictionary.com/chase+your+tail

Flego, L. (2016). A woman who cuts her hair is planning changes in her
life. Retrieved from https://gracefulstory.com/fashion-
beauty/woman-cuts-hair-planning-changes-life/

Funai E.F., et al. Management of normal labor and delivery.
https://www.uptodate.com/contents/search. Accessed June 16,
2016.

Gabbe S.G., et al. Normal labor and delivery. In: Obstetrics: Normal and
Problem Pregnancies. 7th ed. Philadelphia, Pa.: Saunders Elsevier;
2016. http://www.clinicalkey.com. Accessed June 16, 2016.

Guldner, Dr. (2020). Long Distance Relationship Statistics. Retrieved from
https://www.longdistancerelationshipstatistics.com/

Haynes, B. K. (n.d.). Seven Keys to Unlocking the Power of Your Vision.
Retrieved from https://leadtoimpact.com/seven-keys-to-
unlocking-the-power-of-your-vision/

MacDonald, W. (2016). Believer's Bible Commentary. Retrieved from
https://www.biblegateway.com/passage/?search=Ps 37:1-Ps
37:40

Phoenix, O. (2013). Olga Phoenix Project: Healing for Social Change.
Retrieved from http://www.olgaphoenix.com/wp-
content/uploads/2015/05/SelfCare-Wheel-Final.pdf

Satin A.J. Latent phase of labor.
https://www.uptodate.com/contents/search. Accessed June 16,
2016.

Simkin P. et al. Nonpharmacological approaches to management of labor pain. https://www.uptodate.com/contents/search. Accessed June 16, 2016.

Spafford, H.G. (1873). It Is Well With My Soul. Retrieved from https://www.blueletterbible.org/hymns/i/It_Is_Well_With_My_Soul.cfm

Younger Meek J, et al. The first feedings. In: New Mother's Guide to Breastfeeding. 2nd ed. New York, N.Y.: Bantam Books.

Made in the USA
Middletown, DE
05 September 2022

72486413R00071